THE VEGETARIAN GOURMET

THE VEGETARIAN GOURMET

CENTURY HUTCHINSON
LONDON

This edition published 1986
by Century Hutchinson Ltd
Brookmount House,
62-65 Chandos Place
London WC2N 4NW

Recipes in this book have previously appeared in the
following books by David Scott:
The Japanese Cookbook, Barrie and Jenkins (1979)
Grains, Beans and Nuts, Hutchinson (1980)
Middle Eastern Vegetarian Cookery, Hutchinson (1981)
Traditional Arab Cookery, Hutchinson (1983)
Indonesian Cookery, Hutchinson (1984)
Protein for Vegetarians, Hutchinson (1985)
The Vegan Diet, Century Hutchinson (1985)

ISBN 0-7126-9535-4

Edited, designed and produced by
The Paul Press Ltd, 22 Bruton Street, London W1X 7DA

Project Editor Morag Neil
Designers David Ayers, Joanna Walker
Photography Jon Bouchier
Cookery Joyce Harrison
Stylist Jessica Georgiadis

Art Director Stephen McCurdy
Editorial Director Jeremy Harwood
Publishing Director Nigel Perryman

Typeset by Wordsmiths, Street, Somerset
Origination by Gee & Watson, Sutton, Surrey
Printed and bound in the Netherlands by Royal Smeets
Offset BV, Weert

CONTENTS

Introduction

The Vegetarian Gourmet is planned to be exactly what its title implies – a practical commonsense gourmet guide to vegetarian cookery, its aim being to place its subject firmly in the context of the family kitchen. In planning it, I have kept two main aims firmly in mind.

The first of these aims applies to any good vegetarian cookery book. My intention is to offer you a straightforward guide to how, and why, we can enjoy a healthy, balanced and high quality protein diet without eating meat or fish. As well as protein, the body needs a balance of carbohydrates, vitamins and minerals; these needs have also been considered in the recipes I have selected for inclusion in this book. The second aim is to offer you a truly varied selection of vegetarian dishes from across the world – all of them easy to prepare and delicious to eat – so that you can discover, through experience, that vegetarian dishes can stand alongside any other form of cuisine.

Regardless of whether you are experimenting with vegetarian cooking for the first time or not, read the opening section first, as this will help you understand the principles behind the recipes that follow, as well as giving you lots of useful tips and hints. Then, try the recipes themselves, but, when you do so, remember one cardinal rule. In the last analysis, finding the right diet for your needs depends on your own awareness of how the foods you eat affect you. The best diet is naturally the one that makes you feel good, alert, and glad to be you.

GOURMET BASICS

This book is dedicated to the proposition that gourmet vegetarian cooking is not cranky and time-consuming – it is an art well within any cook's grasp. The introductory section that follows is planned to outline some of the key basics – from the importance of balancing your diet to the qualities of the various grains, pulses and nuts that will play an vital part in your vegetarian regime. In addition, there are buying, preparation and cooking hints, plus a basic menu planner.

THE BALANCED DIET

GENERAL RULES FOR A HEALTHY DIET

A varied diet of natural foods composed mainly of whole grains or whole grain products, fresh vegetables and fruits, dried (not tinned) pulses, unhydrogenated vegetable oils, nuts, seeds and dairy products in moderation, will supply all the nutrients you need. Natural foods taste better than refined foods and their nutrient and fibre content is always higher. A diet composed mainly of refined foods, often full of sugar and additives, saturated fats and too much salt, is definitely bad for your health. However, having said that, it does no harm to eat a slice of white bread or have more cream than you really need just occasionally.

Moderation and self-awareness of your own needs are the touchstones of a good diet. An obsession with proper eating, like an obsession with overeating, causes tension and bad digestion.

For growth, maintenance, energy, repair and regulation of metabolic processes the body needs proteins, carbohydrates, fats, vitamins and minerals. For a healthy and energy-giving diet, all five groups are needed in the right balance. Proteins are needed for growth, repair and maintenance of bodily tissues. Carbohydrates and fats provide energy for the body's activities, while fats are also the source of the fat-soluble vitamins A, D, E, and K. Vitamins and minerals are required in very small amounts, but they are essential to the efficient functioning and regulation of all the body's processes.

PROTEINS

The proteins the body needs are composed of twenty-two amino acids. Eight of these acids, called the essential amino acids (EAA) cannot be synthesized by the body and must be contained in the food we eat. All eight EAA are required simultaneously and each must be in the correct proportion to the others if the body is to use them efficiently. Fortunately for us, food proteins normally contain all eight EAA, although one or more may be present in a disproportionately small amount. This small amount of one amino acid limits the usable amount of the remaining essential amino acids, since the body must be provided with them all at the same time in exactly the right profile. The EAA in short supply is called the limiting EAA and it affects the biological value (the percentage of protein present that can be utilized) of a particular foodstuff. Fortunately the amino acid in short supply in one food is often available in excess in another.

By combining two or more complementary foods in one meal we obtain protein of much higher quality or biological value than the total obtained from eating the foods separately. For instance, most grains (e.g. rice, wheat, corn) or grain products are high in the amino acid tryptophan, but low in lysine, while most pulses (e.g. beans, peas, lentils) are high in lysine and low in tryptophan. Thus a dish containing, say, rice and lentils would supply protein of higher biological value than the same total weight of rice or lentils alone.

The main sources of protein for vegetarians are grains, pulses, milk, milk products (e.g. cheese and yoghurt), eggs, nuts and seeds.

The combinations of vegetarian food groups that advantageously complement their individual biological values are:

1. Milk, cheese, yoghurt, or other milk products, either in or with any dish containing grains, pulses, nuts or seeds.
2. Grains, either whole or as a flour product either in or with any dish containing pulses or dairy products.
3. Pulses, either in or with any dish containing grains, dairy products or nuts and seeds.

CARBOHYDRATES

Carbohydrates are the body's main source of energy. They are present in foods such as starches and sugars. Starch is obtained from cereal grains and their products, pulses, vegetables (especially root vegetables), and nuts. The complex combination of starches and protein in these foods is a good one for people involved in manual work or sport. Naturally occurring sugars are found in fruits, honey and milk. Refined sugar, added liberally to so many foods, should be used moderately. It lacks every nutrient except carbohydrate and it tends, by spoiling the appetitie, to displace from the diet other foods containing the nutrients we need.

FATS

Fats provide a concentrated energy source and the essential fat-soluble vitamins A, D and E. Every fat or oil contains active (unsaturated) or inactive (saturated) acids or both. The active acids are called essential fatty acids (EFA). They are contained in the polyunsaturated fats recommended by many authorities over saturated fats with the aim of helping to prevent heart disease. The saturated fats we eat come generally from animal sources such as meat, butter, cream or cheese. In the recipes in this book, vegetable oils (sunflower, olive, safflower and sesame seed oils are the best), polyunsaturated margarines and low fat cheeses or other milk products are recommended when possible. Fats of any description, particularly saturated fats, should be used in only moderate amounts. A considerable body of specialists are now of the opinion that the risk of heart disease, high blood pressure and some cancers can be reduced by cutting saturated fat intake. Incidentally, lacto-vegetarians probably have a higher intake of saturated fats than vegans, but a lower one than meat eaters.

FIBRE

Fibre is found in unrefined cereals, fruit and vegetables. It is not a nutrient because it is not digested, but, because it adds bulk to the body's waste products, it is essential to their efficient elimination and therefore a healthy digestive system. Experts believe that there may be a link between a low intake of fibre in the typical western diet and high rates of cancer and heart disease. The concensus of opinion is that we should eat just over 1oz (30g) per day of dietary fibre. By eating fewer refined foods and more fresh fruit and vegetables this happens naturally.

SIX-POINT PLAN FOR A HEALTHY DIET

By keeping these six simple points in mind each time you are buying food in a shop or market or eating in a restaurant, you can choose the healthiest of what is available:

MORE fibre

MORE fresh fruit and vegetables

LESS salt

LESS sugar

LESS fat

WATCH the calories

VITAMINS AND MINERALS

The body cannot synthesize the vitamins and minerals it requires, so they must be supplied in the food we eat. The vitamins and minerals are an unrelated group of substances, but their functions in the body are interrelated and they are all required in the right balance.

Fresh fruits and vegetables are also prime sources of vitamin C, Vitamin A (as carotene), floic acid, vitamin E, vitamin K and a wide range of minerals. As a good rule of thumb, you should eat some fruits and vegetables at every meal. Preferably eat them raw, or cook them for the minimum of time and in as little water as possible, for nutrients such as vitamins and minerals are leeched out into the water during cooking (e.g. when boiling potatoes) and will be lost unless you keep and use the cooking water.

A mixed diet of whole grains, pulses, dairy products, vegetables, including salads and fresh fruits, will normally provide all the vitamins and minerals we need.

THE VEGAN DIET AND NUTRITION

Vegans do not eat milk, cheese, butter, eggs, or foods that contain them. The question that most often bothers people about the vegan diet is whether it will provide enough protein. The question has been answered in the affirmative, both academically and practically by the active and varied lives of many practising vegans and peoples who, because of where they live in the world and/or cultural traditon, follow a vegan diet naturally. So, there is no reason for a vegan diet not to work for you.

A mixed diet of whole grains and flours, pulses (including sprouted varieties such as mung beans, alfalfa, lentils), nuts, seeds, vegetables (both raw and lightly cooked) vegetable derivitives, such as plant milks (e.g. soya), and fresh fruit provides low-fat, wholesome nutrients not denatured by overcooking and uncontaminated with the additives and saturated fats present in many refined foods, meats and dairy produce.

If you are attracted to this type of diet, remember that balance is all-important. To ensure a good protein balance, the source of the protein should be about 60 per cent grains, 35 per cent pulses and/or nuts and seeds and 5 per cent leafy green vegetables. These figures only relate to protein requirements, so you must remember that, in order to take in the other nutrients you need, your diet must also include vegetables (especially raw) and fruit.

GRAINS

Grains are embryonic plants and are literally small packages of nourishment and energy and they provide the world with its principal food source. Since they contain protein, carbohydrate and many vitamins in excellent proportion for our particular nutritional needs, they are fine foods.

The grain family comprises over 5000 species. Amongst these can be found the world's principal cereal crops: barley, maize (corn), oats, rice, rye and wheat. Until recently, particular staple grains have been associated with certain parts of the world: rice with east Asia, wheat with the West, maize (corn) with the Americas. Nowadays,with a few exceptions, these divisions are less clear rice, for instance, is as common in Europe as bread is in Japan. The exceptions stand out: sorghum and millet, for instance, are the staple grains of much of Africa, but sorghum is virtually unknown in the West, where millet is fed mainly to caged birds!

BUYING AND COOKING GRAINS

If possible, buy organically grown grains and always whole, unrefined varieties – go for brown rather than white rice. All the grains are very good cooked on their own in water and then served as a side dish to vegetables and/or a sauce, or combined with raw vegetables and made into a salad. Cooked grains can also be mixed with other ingredients and baked or used to stuff vegetables or make rissoles. Some grains benefit from dry roasting before boiling in water and this is particularly the case with buckwheat (kasha).

To cook grains add one part of grain to two to three parts of boiling, slightly salted water. Bring back to the boil, reduce the heat, cover the pan with a closely-fitting lid and simmer gently until all the water is absorbed and the grains are tender.

BARLEY

The widespread cultivation of wheat and rice has led to a gradual worldwide decline in the importance of barley and nowadays it is principally cultivated for use in brewing and for animal food, although it is well suited to human consumption and can be used to make flat breads and cakes, porridges, soups and stews. Wholegrain barley contains an average eleven per cent by weight of protein which compares well with wheat and rice, valuable B vitamins and important minerals.

BUCKWHEAT

Although buckwheat is commonly regarded as a grain, it is in fact the seed of a herbacious plant. The hulled buckwheat grain or kasha as it is sometimes called, loses some of its flavour if it is not dry roasted before cooking. To do this, heat a pan over medium-high heat (do not add oil), pour in the kasha and stir the grains around in the pan with a wooden spoon until they start to brown a little. Remove the pan from the heat. The kasha is now ready for cooking.

Kasha has an interesting, nutty flavour and it makes a pleasant change from the regular grains. It is served both as a side dish like potatoes or rice and as an ingredient in savoury dishes. The crushed seeds (called groats) cook more quickly than kasha. They are used in the same way or in sweet dishes and breakfast cereals to add crunchiness. Buckwheat flour is used to make pancakes, muffins, cakes and pasta. The flour is rather heavy and expensive and is usually mixed with lighter, cheaper flours. It contains valuable amounts of vitamins and minerals and, on average, eleven per cent by weight of protein.

CORN (MAIZE)

The corn or maize plant belongs to the grass family and of the five main varieties grown commercially, sweet corn or corn on the cob (from which frozen or tinned corn kernels are obtained) and cornmeal are the types probably best known to cooks. Corn grain is not as nutritionally complete as whole rice or wholewheat. However, whole corn kernels or whole cornmeal is more nutritious than either white rice or white flour and eaten in combination with other foods, particularly pulses, it is an excellent food. Popcorn is poor nutritionally and should really only be considered as fun food.

TYPES OF MAIZE FLOUR

Whole maize or cornmeal retains all the goodness of the corn. Stoneground is the best if you can obtain it. Polenta is the Italian name for yellow maize or cornmeal. It is a staple food in parts of northern Italy where boiled polenta, cooled and then fired sometimes takes the place of bread. **Cornflour** is not as nutritious as whole maize flour, but excellent for thickening soups, sauces, etc.

Hominy flour or grits is an old American food, sometimes called samp, which is made by treating kernels or corn with lye, which dissolves the skin. They are then washed, boiled and finally dried. Hominy grits are made by coarsely milling dried hominy, which should then be soaked overnight before cooking.

OATS

Although oats are a tasty food and a rich source of nutrients, they still contribute very little to our overbalanced Western diets. Whole oat grain is generally equal to or richer than either whole wheat or rice. The grain is a good source of B vitamins and minerals.

Oatmeal grains or groats as they are sometimes called, are usually sold as oatmeal or oatmeal flour. They are principally used as breakfast foods (e.g. in porridge, muesli) and for the making of breads, cakes, and scones, but they can also be used in savoury dishes, soups and stews.

MUESLI

Muesli was formulated by Swiss nutritionist Dr Bircher-Benner over 70 years ago. The recipe was devised to provide a food that supplied good amounts of protein, vitamins, minerals and roughage without overloading the body with too much rich food. Muesli is considered by most nutritionists to be an excellent food combination.

RICE

Nearly half the world's population depends on rice as their staple food and a fair proportion of this number rely almost solely on rice for their nutritional needs. In its least processed form, that of brown rice, it is an excellent source of B complex vitamins, vitamin E and certain minerals.

We have the choice of eating nutritious brown rice or refined white rice. In the west this choice is not so important, since most of us have a mixed diet that probaby supplies our nutritional needs. There is, however, one element that may be missing from our diet, and that's fibre. If your diet is heavily dependent on refined foods you would be wise to start including in it some wholefoods, such as brown rice.

TYPES OF RICE

Brown rice is rice minus its hull or husk; contains all nutrients naturally present in the grain. It takes longer to cook than white rice and needs more water. Pale brown in colour and slightly chewy with a nutty flavour.

Converted or par boiled rice is prepared from rice that has been soaked, steamed and dried before hulling and milling. It contains most of its original nutrients.

Rice flakes are white rice flaked in a power mill. Prepared for its quick cooking properties. Often used in soups and puddings. Brown rice flakes are now available.

Rice flour is white rice ground into flour and used in puddings, sauces, confectionary, pasta and bread making (mixed with wheat flour).

Long grain rice is often called patna rice, since it is thought to have originated from Patna in India. When cooked, the grains separate and become light and fluffy. Excellent for serving on its own as well as in pilaffs, risottos and other savoury dishes.

Medium grain rice is shorter than patna rice, but the grains are a little more plump. Basmatti rice from India is of medium length but much thinner than the patna variety.

Short grain rice is a short plump grain rice, most popular in Japan and parts of China. It's quite sticky when cooked and in the west is usually reserved for making puddings. It is, however, well suited to being eaten with chopsticks, which may account for its popularity in Japan, where it is served plain and unsalted as an accompaniment to a savoury dish.

Italian rice is another short-grain variety. The grain absorbs more water than other types of rice, and is used for making dishes such as risotto in which the sauce is cooked in with the rice. Arborio rice is considered to be the best.

White rice has the hulls, germ and most of the bran layers removed, resulting in considerable loss of nutrients (sometimes these are re-added artificially).

Wild rice is a cereal grain native to North America, China and Japan. The plant is difficult to grow domestically, and is consequently expensive. Nutritionally it's very rich and contains more protein and vitamins than regular rice. Raw wild rice is brown, but it acquires a faint purplish colour when cooked. It has a delicate nutty flavour.

COOKING RICE

The cooking qualities of rice differ considerably depending on the source of the rice, its age and whether it is long or short grain, but the following general rules are useful:8oz (225g) uncooked rice gives about 1½lb (700g) cooked rice. One volume of uncooked rice gives three volumes of cooked rice2-3oz (50-70g) uncooked rice per person is an average serving.

One volume of uncooked rice requires two volumes of water to cook in. Washing rice causes a loss of nutrients and European or American packed white rice requires only light rinsing before cooking. Asian packed or loose rice and brown rice should be well rinsed. If the rice has been rinsed before cooking it is not necessary to do so again afterwards.

RYE

Much of today's rye is grown for making rye whiskey or is ground into flour for bread making. The flour contains less gluten than wheat flour and consequently rises less in the breadmaking process. Rye bread is flatter and more filling than yeasted wheat bread and it has a more distinctive taste and denser texture. Dark rye flour is prepared from the whole grain while the lighter coloured rye flour has had some of the bran removed.

Whole rye grains or groats may be used in the same ways as whole wheat grains or brown rice, while cracked rye (grits or flakes) cook more quickly and are useful in stews, soups and cake making.

Whole rye grains or flour are an excellent source of vitamins, minerals and the protein content compares well with rice, wheat and corn.

WHEAT

There are numerous ways of cooking wheat and wheat flour products. The variety of cooking methods has, of course, resulted from regional differences, types of wheat available, cultural traditions, the influence of technology and, not least, human inventiveness.

BULGAR OR BURGHUL WHEAT

This is parboiled, cracked wheat. Although relatively unknown in the west, bulgar is the staple food of some countries of the Middle East, where it is served with rice and also used as the basis for a variety of cold salads. Bulgar has all the nutritional qualities of wholewheat grain. It has a distinctive taste and is easy to cook.

SEMOLINA

Semolina is produced from the starchy endosperm of the wheat grain. It is milled in various grades to give fine, medium or coarse semolina. Fine semolina is used in puddings and pasta production, while coarse semolina is used to make couscous.

Couscous is probably the most common and most widely known North African Arab dish in which the grains are steamed over a rich sauce or stew and then served in a mountainous heap with the sauce poured over. Couscous is never cooked in the sauce. Traditionally the stew is made with mutton or chicken, though a vegetable variation is just as tasty (see p85). A special pot called a couscousier is traditionally used for cooking the stew and simultaneously steaming the couscous, but a saucepan with a snug-fitting colander on top will serve just as well.

Pasta, Italian style, is made from a dough of wheat flour, eggs and water. The dough is rolled out and cut into any of a huge variety of shapes, then dried before cooking in water. The best pasta is made from hard grained wheats, particularly durum wheat.

Wholemeal pasta is more nutritious and is higher in protein than normal white flour pasta.

When cooking pasta the important rule is to use a large pot and plenty of water. Generally 1lb (450g) pasta needs 6 pints (3 litres) water. For salt, 1½ tablespoons per 1lb (450g) pasta is an average amount, added after the water has boiled and before the pasta is put in. To prevent the pasta sticking to itself during cooking, a little butter or oil is added to the water. Thus, the water is brought to a rolling boil, salted, about 2 tablespoons oil are added and the pasta is then carefully fed into the pot and boiled, uncovered, until it is soft on the outside but with a slight resistance at the centre, al dente. Cooking times vary depending on the type of pasta, and whether it is bought or home-made. Shop bought pasta cooks in less than five minutes.

As soon as the pasta is cooked, drain it in a colander and serve with a sauce a grated cheese or on its own dressed with melted butter or olive oil and seasoned with freshly milled black pepper.

WHEAT FLOUR

Soft wheat has a lower protein content, and thus less gluten than hard wheat; it is usually winter-sown and grown in moist, temperate conditions. The flour it gives is good for making cakes and biscuits.

Hard grained wheat contains more protein, and thus more gluten, which makes it excellent for bread and pasta. It is spring-sown, and harvested in warm, dry conditions. American and Canadian wheats are often of this type. In practice, hard and soft wheats are frequently blended to provide flour for specific purposes. The protein, vitamins and minerals in wheat are distributed throughout the grain, but a substantial proportion of the nutrients are contained in the outer edges. It is this portion of the grain that is removed when the grain is milled.

BROWN AND WHITE BREAD

To get the best nutritional value out of wheat, we should buy or make bread from 100 per cent wholemeal flour milled on stone rollers. This does not take the question of taste or appetite into account, however!

LEAVENED BREAD

Leavened bread can be made from any sort of wheat flour, but to make bread with a fine texture and a good satisfying taste it is best to use a hard (also called strong) flour. These are flours with a high gluten content and they give a firm elastic dough. You may use either strong brown or strong white flour, depending upon your preference and the type of bread you wish to make. Stoneground 100 per cent wholemeal flour makes the most nutritious and filling bread. For a lighter, less chewy bread, but one which still retains most of the goodness of the wheat, use wheatmeal of 81 to 85 per cent extraction. For the times when you wish to make a light-textured bread, use a strong white flour of a low extraction.

UNLEAVENED (UNYEASTED) BREAD

Unleavened or unyeasted bread is made by mixing flour, salt and water to form dough which is shaped into a loaf or rolled out into a flat round and baked. In the past, since it can be cooked more quickly than leavened bread, this type of bread has been more common in areas of the world where fuel was not easily available. In recent times it has become more widely popular, and is particularly recommended by the macrobiotic movement.

In India and Pakistan, the most common form of bread is the flat, unleavened, round chapatti. The wheat grain is ground locally on stone mills, and the flour produced is quite coarse. In the West, special chapatti flour can be obtained from Indian provision stores.

Another well-known unleavened bread is the tortilla from Mexico. Tortillas are made from a cornmeal and wholemeal wheat flour mixture and are a staple of Latin American cookery, tasting particularly delicious when filled with various spicy mixtures.

WHOLEWHEAT

Cooked wholewheat grains (sometimes called berries) make surprisingly tasty and satisfying dishes, and eating the whole grain ensures you get all the nutritious goodness of the wheat. Wholewheat can also be used to make excellent salads if mixed with salad vegetables and dressing or with cooked beans. The latter mixture is an especially rich protein combination.

The grains are prepared for cooking by soaking in water for three to four hours. They are then cooked in the same way as brown rice. Wholewheat is far more fibrous than rice, however, and never cooks to the same softness. For this reason it is much harder to overcook wholewhaet than rice. In most dishes where you would use brown rice, wholewheat can be substituted.

To make enough plain.boiled wholewheat for four, you need 1lb (450g) of soaked and drained wholewheat berries. Bring 2 pints (1.1 litres) of water to a rolling boil, add the wheat to the water and return the mixture to the boil. Then, reduce the heat and allow the mixture to simmer for 1½ hours – or until the wheat is cooked to the softness you personally require. Add 1 teaspoon of salt towards the end of the cooking time.

To speed up the cooking time, dry-roast the wheat in a hot frying pan for two to three minutes before adding it to the boiling water.

PULSES

Dried beans, peas and lentils, collectively called pulses, are a rich source of protein, carbohydrate and some vitamins and minerals. Correctly soaked and cooked, pulses are easily digested and, in this section, detailed soaking and cooking hints are given, plus tips on buying.

Beans, peas and lentils cooked on their own can be used in salads, soups and stuffings, or puréed to make dips and spreads. Mixed with cooked grains thay make a particularly nutritious combination.

SOAKING PULSES

Most pulses should be soaked befoire cooking to ensure they are digestible. The usual soaking times are 12 to 24 hours, although there is a quicker soaking method (discussed below).

LONGER SOAKING METHOD

Weigh out the beans you require (8oz/225g serves about 4 people). Cover the beans in water (1½ pints/850ml water per 8oz/225g beans). Leave them according to their recommended soaking times – these vary from two to three hours in the case of Aduki beans to overnight in the majority of other cases. This means leaving the beans to soak for at least eight to 12 hours.

QUICK SOAKING METHOD

Weigh out the beans, put in a heavy saucepan and cover with water as directed in the long soaking method. Cover the pot and bring to the boil, reduce the heat and simmer for five minutes. Remove the pot from the heat and leave the beans to soak for the appropriate time – on average, this is 2-3 hours. After this time bring the beans back to the boil in the same water and cook them until tender. Whichever soaking method you use, the cooking time remains the same – up to 2 hours if you are not using a pressure cooker and considerably less if you are.

COOKING TIPS

Do not add salt to the beans until near the end of the

cooking time, otherwise they harden and take longer to cook than they would otherwise.

- Other seasonings should be added later as well, as beans, while cooking, seem to absorb and neutralize flavours. Lentils and split peas are the exception to this rule and can be seasoned at the start of cooking.
- If a bean dish is to be reheated the following day, check the seasoning and add before serving if necessary.
- Do not add bicarbonate of soda to the cooking water. It's not needed and destroys vitamins.
- Water in which beans have been cooked makes excellent stock.

ADUKI BEANS

This seed or bean is small, shiny and red and it is most popular in the far eastern countries of Japan, Korea and China. It has a sweet taste and apart from its use in savoury dishes, the cooked mashed beans are used as a sweet filling in cakes and buns.

BLACK BEANS

A black, shiny bean popular in South America and the Caribbean. They are slightly sweet and particularly good in soups and casseroles. In the Caribbean they are traditionally flavoured with cumin, garlic and a spicy tomato sauce. The smaller variety popular in China, are normally fermented with salt and served in quantities with fish or chicken. Black bean sauce is also a popular Chinese accompaniment to main dishes (it is sometimes made from soya beans).

BLACK-EYED BEANS (COW PEAS)

White or creamy bean with a black or dark yellow eye. The plant is native to Africa but now widely cultivated in India, China and the Americas. Black-eyed beans, pork and sweet potato are said to be a splendid combination.

BROAD BEANS

Either a creamy white or brown variety available. Immature pods can be eaten as vegetables as can the young green beans. The mature dried beans need a good soaking and long cooking before use. They are popular in casseroles, salads, puréed or in pies.

BUTTER BEANS (LIMA BEANS)

These beans are now cultivated in tropical areas all over the world. They are a good accompaniment to pork or poultry or combined with sweetcorn to make the traditional American dish succotash, or in soups, casseroles, puréed or served with sour cream in salads.

CHICK-PEAS (GARBANZOS)

This is my favourite bean. It is native to the Mediterranean region but now grows throughout the sub-tropics. The peas are normally yellow but are sometimes creamy white or brown with a dimpled surface. They are most famous as an ingredient of humus in which the cooked peas are ground to a paste mixed with sesame-seed paste (tahini), garlic, lemon, oil and salt and served with pitta bread. Or as falafel in which ground chick-peas are flavoured with onion, parsely, cumin, coriander then rolled into walnut size balls and deep fried.

KIDNEY BEANS

This species of bean is the most commonly cultivated in the worls today and includes all the various type of haricot beans. It is from this group that the famous and ubiquitous baked beans in tomato sauce are prepared.

The following all belong to the kidney bean family:

Borlotti beans are grown in Kenya and Italy and are popular in Italian cooking. They may be reddish, brown or white. They are the main ingredient in which borlottis are cooked with ham bone and spices and served with noodles and topped up with parmesan cheese.

Canellini are small white haricot beans from Argentina. They have a slightly nutty flavour.

Egyptian kidney beans (ful medames) is a very tasty bean but needs long soaking and cooking. In Egypt they are a national dish and they even have ful (Egyptian for 'bean') cafés. Traditionally they are boiled with cumin and served seasoned with garlic, lemon, oil, chopped parsely and chopped boiled egg.

Fagioli are Italian white haricot beans.

Flageolets are a delicate, pale green, young haricot bean with a subtle taste. Grown in France and Italy and usually only available outside these countries tinned.

Haricot beans are a small, tender white bean. The main ingredient in many traditional dishes including cassoulet and cholent. Similar or the same as the American navy bean, Great Northern bean and other beans called white beans.

Pearl beans are a small haricot bean.

Pink beans are grown in Mexico and are often refried (see Pinto bean).

The Pinto bean is a speckled brown bean from Mexico. Used in chilli dishes instead of red kidney beans. It is cooked in large quantities and then refried for later use. Known as refried beans (Frijoles refritos in Mexican).

Red kidney beans are also known as Mexican or chilli beans. Theay are very popular in chilli con carne, soups and salads, and in Spain and Japan when served with white rice.

LENTILS

Lentils are available in a variety of sizes and colours, although the red, green and brown types are the most easily found in the West. Red lentils are often sold split for easier cooking. Chinese varieties are generally smaller than Indian lentils. Lentils cook quickly and need little or no soaking although some people believe soaking increases their digestibility. They have a higher protein content than most other legumes and high carbohydrate content. They provide good food for cold days or labour-intensive work.

MUNG BEAN

A small, highly nutritious olive-green bean. The mung plant grows quickly and several crops a year can be harvested. For this reason it is excellent for growing bean sprouts and in China the beans are used solely for sprouting. The bean sprouts most commonly available commercially in both Britain and the USA are grown from mung beans.

PEAS

Nowadays, fresh, frozen or tinned peas are much more common than the dried variety, although split peas are still popular. There are two main types of common pea. The first and most popular for human consumption is the garden pea with which we are all familiar. The second is the field pea, considered inferior in taste to the garden pea and grown as animal food. Garden peas available commercially have been separated into size and shape and are sold according to their sweetness and starch content. Thus we have sugar peas, snow peas, petits pois and marrowfat peas ranging from the sweet to the starchy marrow fats.

Yellow split peas are used in soups, casseroles and in India like lentils for preparing dhal and rissoles.

Green split peas are good in soups, stews and casseroles.

PEANUTS (GROUND NUTS)

The peanut is strictly speaking, a legume and not a nut. It's best known to us in its salted and roasted form as a snack food, although it's grown principally as a source of vegetable oil.

Peanuts contain a high proportion of essential fatty acids and peanut butter should be a nutritious food. Unfortunately to increase the shelf life of their product manufacturers hydrogenate the butter and thus turn its essential oils into fats good only for providing calories. It's worth buying it from a reputable wholefood store.

PIGEON PEAS (GUNGAR PEAS)

Small, round, flat peas speckled with brown marks. The plant originated in South East Asia but is now most popular in India where its drought-resisting properties are very useful. It is also popular in the Caribbean where together with rice it forms part of the staple diet. The young seeds can be eaten fresh as a vegetable or dried and used like lentils.

SOYA BEANS

Soya beans are the most nutritious of all the legumes. They contain as much high-quality protein as steak and further contain unsaturated fats that can reduce cholesterol levels in the blood.

Soya bean products:
The three main soya bean products are bean curd (tofu), miso (bean paste), and soy sauce (shoya). Bean curd or tofu is a fermented soya bean product, it is white and has the consistency of a delicate custard. Fried bean curd develops a tougher outer coat and can be used in salads, as a side dish or in the same way that cheese is often used. It is a rich source of protein and minerals, contains no fat and is an aid to digestion.

Miso is a fermented soya bean paste that keeps indefinitely; its flavour even improves with age. Combined with rice or other grains, miso supplies all the essential amino acids and also contains enzymes that are helpful to the digestion process. It is a versatile ingredient and is used as a base for soups, salad dressings and sauces, as a marinade for fish, meat or vegetables or as a spread.

Soy sauce is the best-known soya bean product. Real soy sauce is made from a mixture of soya beans, wheat and salt, fermented together for up to two years, then mashed and filtered. Tamari is a brand name for real soy sauce.

In the east soya beans are not usually soaked and boiled whole as with other legumes, but then there is no great tradition for casserole type dishes in this part of the world and whole dried soya beans lend themselves best to this style of cooking.

FRESH SOYA MILK

Rinse ¼lb (100g) beans and soak them in 1 pint (0.5 l) water for ten hours or overnighjt. Wash well. Put the beans in a blender with very hot water, allowing about 1 pint (0.5 l) of water to 1 cup of beans. Blend well. Repeat until all the beans have been liquidized. Bring the liquid slowly to the boil in a large heavy saucepan, stirring frequently to prevent sticking. Watch it carefully because it will easily boil over. (The quantities given here will make 2 pints (1.1l) milk.

NUTS

In general, nuts are a delicious and highly nutritious food, whether eaten raw on their own, or used as part of a recipe. To blanche them, put them in a pan of boiling water and allow to stand for two to three minutes (longer for hazelnuts, cobnuts and filberts). Drain, rinse in cold water and rub off the skins.

ALMONDS

Almonds are possibly the most popular of nuts commonly available. Two types of almonds are grown. One is bitter and the other is sweet, and it is the latter variety we are most familiar with. Bitter almonds are most often used for the production of almond oil although occasionally they are called for in recipes in which a bitter flavour is required. Sweet almonds are used extensively in Middle Eastern and Indian cooking. They can be cooked whole or used ground in puddings, cakes and pastries (e.g. marzipan is a mixture of almond paste and sugar).

These nuts can sometimes be shelled with a twist of the fingers, otherwise, if the shell is too hard, a sharp tap with a hammer is normally enough to break it. To remove the brown skin from the nut itself, drop the nuts into boiling water for five minutes, drain, rinse in cold water and the skin will just slip off.

BRAZIL NUTS

Brazil-nut trees are native to the tropical regions of Brazil where the nuts are collected on a commercial scale. They are also found in the forests of Venezuela and Bolivia but not in commercially viable numbers.

Brazil nuts have been popular since Victorian times as a dessert nut, eaten either raw or salted, with a glass of port after dinner. In more recent years they have become popular in the manufacture of chocolates and chocolate bars. There are however, a number of other culinary ways in which they may be used and they are also a rich source of protein, unsaturated fats and vitamin B1.

Brazils are easily shelled after being chilled in the refrigerator for a day or two. Use a nut cracker or a small hammer.

CASHEW NUTS

Cashew nut trees are native to Brazil; the name cashew is

derived from the Brazilian Indian word acaju, which Portugese explorers mispronounced as caju.

The nut is enclosed in a shell which contains an acid fluid harmful to the skin and the nuts are always both shelled and slightly roasted to ensure all vestiges of the fluid are removed before consumption. Cashew nuts have a well balanced combination of proteins, fats and carbohydrates and they are a particularly nutritious food.

HAZELNUTS, COBNUTS AND FILBERTS

Hazelnuts, cobnuts and filberts are closely related nuts which grow on small trees or shrubs belonging to the Corylus family of plants. Originally they are native to the temperate regions of northern Europe and Asia, but they are now cultivated in many parts of the world.

Hazelnuts can be shelled by hitting the centre of the rounded side of the nut with a light hammer. To skin the nuts, bake them in a moderate oven for 10 to 15 minutes, allow them to cool and then, if the nuts are rolled in a damp cloth, the skin will just slip off. Otherwise drop them into a pan of boiling water and leave them to stand for 5 to 10 minutes. Drain, rinse in cold water and rub off the skins.

The nuts may be eaten fresh, roasted, ground or chopped, and they are widely used commercially in the manufacture of chocolates and other sweets. They have wide application in the kitchen and may be used in salads and main dishes as well as desserts. They are a good source of protein, vitamins, fats and minerals.

PINE NUTS (PIGNOLIAS)

Many different species of pine trees yield edible seeds which are collectively known as pine nuts or pignolias. The nuts grow inside the hard outer casing of the familiar pine cone and they grow unshelled. They are usually white or cream in colour with a soft texture and a flavour of terpentine if unroasted. The pine nuts most commonly available in Europe come from the stone pine, a tree native to Italy which is now cultivated all around the Mediterranean coast.

There are many different types of pine trees with edible seeds grown in North America but this food source has never really been exploited except by native Indians who collected the nuts as a traditional winter food supply.

Pine nuts if cooked with other foods impart a delicious and distinctive flavour and they are most popular in

Middle Eastern and Italian cooking. I find them particularly delicious when sprinkled on top of a gratin dish just before baking or grilling.

PISTACHIO NUTS

The pistachio nut is very popular in America where its pale green colour is most often observed gracing an ice cream cone piled high with pistachio ice cream. However, it has a venerable history and pistachios have been grown in the warmer parts of Asia for thousands of years. They are now cultivated in the Mediterranean countries of Europe, the Middle East, India and on a large scale in the south western states of America.

The nut grows in a thin shell which conveniently cracks open at one end when the nut is ripe. In Europe and America pistachios are normally eaten as dessert nuts or used for decorating sweets and pastries. In Middle Eastern countries they are used as important ingredients in savoury dishes. They are a good source of vitamin A as well as protein, unsaturated fats and minerals.

SWEET CHESTNUTS

The chestnut is a native of the Mediterranean area but it was carried north by the Romans and is now widespread throughout Europe. It was given the name sweet chestnut to prevent confusion with the horse-chestnut tree, a different species; the seeds of the horse-chestnut are not true nuts and they have a bitter unpleasant taste.

In southern Europe, particularly Italy, sweet chestnuts have been a staple food for thousands of years. They are eaten roasted, stewed or dried and ground into flour for bread and porridge making. Most of the chestnuts available for export are produced in France where they grow two categories, the regular chestnut called chataignes and the best quality chestnuts called marrons. It is from the latter that the famous maron glacé, a sweet glazed chestnut, are prepared.

Chestnuts are not such concentrated foods as other nuts and they contain much less protein and fat and more carbohydrates. They are, however, easily digestible and an excellent energy source. Serve them roasted or boiled with vegetables or salad as you may do rice or potatoes. Chestnut flour may be used in cake making and the purée is good in stuffings, sauces and desserts.

Chestnuts are easier to shell and skin after boiling or roasting. Cut two slits in the outer casing on the flat side of each of the nuts and drop them in boiling water for two or three minutes. Drain and leave them to cool. The casing and skin can now be removed with a vegetable knife. Alternatively place the slit chestnuts on a baking tray in a hot oven and cook for 10 minutes or until the slits start to open up. Remove them from the oven and the casing and skin can be easily removed with the help of a knife.

WALNUTS

Walnut trees are native to Iran, but, as with many other plants, they were carried into many parts of Europe by the Romans and they are now widespread. The nut and its shell are the stone inside the green plum-size fruit of the walnut tree.

The black walnut, which is different in shape and flavour and with a much harder shell than the ordinary variety, is native to America. In America the European walnut is known as the English walnut, whilst in Europe it's sometimes known as the Italian walnut.

Walnuts and particularly the black walnut, are a good source of protein, unsaturated fats, vitamins and minerals. The nuts are excellent in pies, stuffings, breads, casseroles, salads and as topping on gratin dishes and cakes. The unripe nut can be pickled and the raw nuts are good with cheese and fruit. The nuts can be shelled by striking the junction of the two halves with a light hammer.

ROASTING NUTS AND SEEDS

Preheat the oven to 325°F (170°C, gas mark 3). Spread the whole or chopped nuts or seeds on a baking tray and place them in the oven. Bake them for about 10 minutes giving them a shake once or twice during this time. The nuts or seeds are ready when lightly browned.

Nuts or seeds may also be pan roasted on top of the oven. Put them in an ungreased, heavy frying pan and gently toss them about over a moderate flame until lightly browned.

For spiced nuts sprinkle the roasting nuts with the following ingredients, well mixed, just before you remove them from the pan or oven. These amounts will do for 1lb (450g) of nuts.

2 teaspoons salt
½ teaspoon ground cumin
½ teaspoon ground cinnamon
½ teaspoon ground ginger
½ teaspoon ground cloves
1 tablespoon brown sugar (optional)

PLANNING MENUS

As a general guide, the main meal of the day should provide approximately 50 per cent of the protein you need, one light meal should provide about 25 per cent and breakfast about 25 per cent. Each meal should contain two or more major protein sources and at least one meal should include two or more lightly cooked fresh vegetables and a fresh salad (including a leafy green vegetable). Fresh fruit (including citrus fruits), three or four times a day, completes the daily requirement.

The list below gives a good indication of protein sources for vegetarians – it is not applicable to vegans, who do not eat dairy products.

SOURCES OF PROTEIN

Grains
Buckwheat and buckwheat flour
Corn and cornmeal
Millet
Rice (brown)
Rolled oats and oatmeal
Rye and rye flour
Wholewheat, wholemeal flour, bulghur (cracked wheat), couscous, wheat germ and bran

Pulses
Aduki beans
Black-eyed beans
Chickpeas (garbanzos)
Kidney beans (including red beans and haricot beans)
Lentils
Peas
Soy beans, soya flour, tofu and miso

Cheeses (low to medium fat)
Cheddar
Cottage cheese
Emmenthal
Gouda
Gruyére
Mozzarella
Parmesan
Ricotta

Nuts
Almonds
Brazils
Cashews
Hazels
Peanuts (classified as a pulse)
Pine nuts (pignolias)
Walnuts

Seeds
Sesame
Sunflower

Dairy products
Eggs
Milk (skimmed milk preferably)
Yoghurt (low fat, natural flavours)

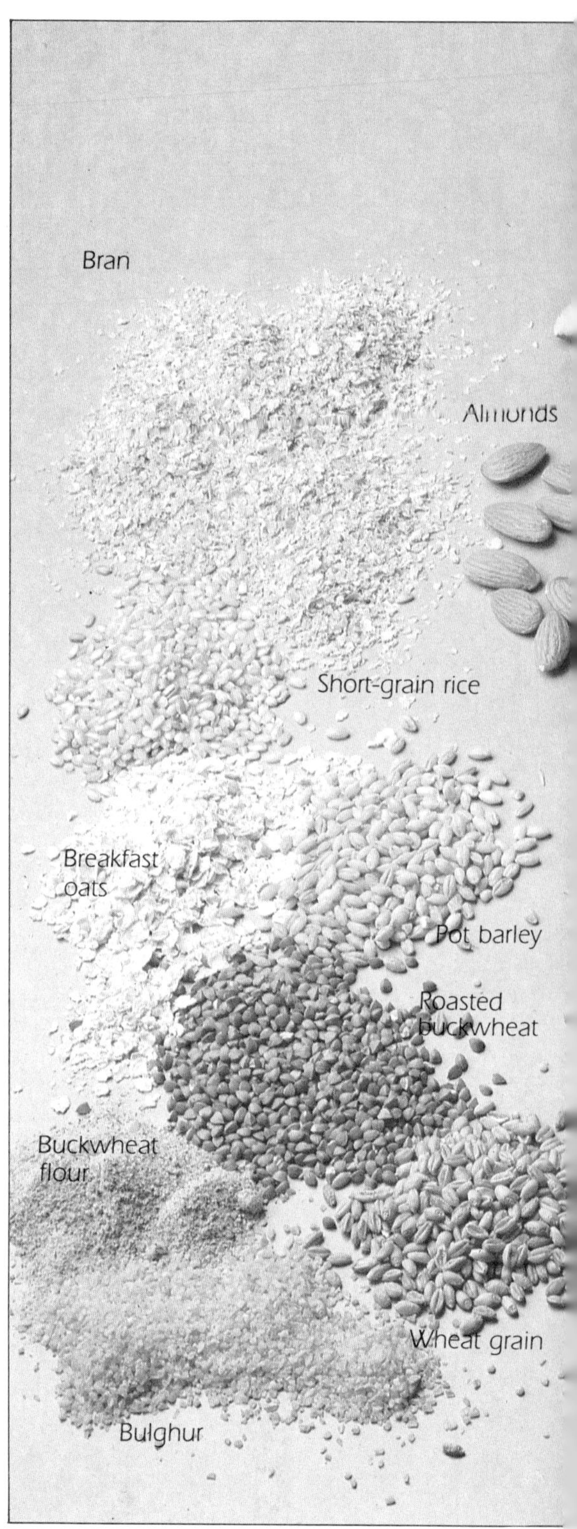

Food for health Some of the wide variety of healthy, protein-packed foods you can eat are shown here.

Milk
Brazils
Gouda
Hazelnuts
Cheddar
Eggs
Cashews
Emmenthal
Sunflower seeds
Aduki beans
Parmesan
Sesame seeds
Whole millet
Green split peas
Chickpeas
Haricot beans
Couscous

THE GOURMET IN ACTION

The recipes in the following chapters of this book are drawn from a world-wide assortment of vegetarian traditions. You will find mouthwatering soups and starters from places as far apart as Japan and Tuscany, main courses from Central Europe, delicious puddings from the Middle East and much, much more. The aim throughout has been to make things clear and simple – little, if any, specialist kitchen equipment is required, while preparation and cooking times are similarly planned to take into account practical timing realities. You will find, for instance, that quite a few gourmet vegetarian dishes actually take less time to prepare than their conventional equivalents.

SOUPS AND STARTERS

This chapter contains fabulous hot and cold soup and starter recipes from all over the world, plus a whole range of attractive dips that you can eat on their own with the appropriate bread or as an attractive accompaniment to a salad. Some of the soups, too, can double up as delicious main courses.

ONION SOUP

This type of onion soup is popular in Iran and Turkey. Its preparation is similar to French onion soup, but the seasoning is different. Alternatively, this soup may be served with croutons and grated cheese. Lightly beaten eggs are whipped into it just before serving.

2oz (50g) butter or vegetable oil
1lb (450g) onions, thinly sliced
3-4pt (1.75-2l) water
1oz (25g) flour
Salt and black pepper to taste
½ teaspoon (2.5ml) turmeric
1 teaspoon (5ml) sugar
Juice of 1 lemon
Slices of French bread and 4oz (100g) Parmesan cheese

Serves 4

Melt the butter or oil in a heavy pan and add the onions. Cook, stirring occasionally for 15 minutes over gentle heat.

Use a little of the water to make a paste with the flour and stir this into the onions. Stirring constantly, continue to cook the onion and flour mixture for 2 to 3 minutes. Add the remaining water and bring to the boil. Reduce heat and season to taste with salt and black pepper. Add the turmeric, sugar and lemon juice, cover and leave to simmer for about 45 minutes. Adjust the seasoning.

Rub the mint to a powder and mix with the cinnamon. Stir the mixture into the soup and remove from the heat. Now stir in the 2 lightly beaten eggs and serve.

Alternatively, leave out the eggs and lightly toast the slices of french bread, put one piece in each bowl, pour the soup over them, and serve with Parmesan cheese.

EGG DROP SOUP

By swirling the soup around as you pour in the beaten egg, you can form beautiful patterns with the strands of cooked egg. The Japanese call these shapes egg-flowers.

2 eggs, beaten
1 tablespoon (15ml) sake or sweet white wine (optional)
Pinch of salt
2 pints (1.1 litres) clear stock
2 teaspoon (10ml) cornflour
1 teaspoon (5ml) soy sauce
4 small leaves spinach, chopped
4 sprigs parsley

Serves 4

Whisk the eggs, add the sake and pinch of salt. Mix the cornflour to a smooth paste with a little of the cold stock.

Bring stock to the boil, pour in the paste and stir in. Add soy sauce and season with salt to taste. Now gradually add beaten egg stirring constantly. Bring to the boil, add the spinach and turn off the heat. Pour into soup bowls and garnish with the parsley.

Delicate appetisers Light soups make excellent starters. The subtle flavours of clear soup with lemon and tofu (left), and egg drop soup (right) will not dull the palate, making them an ideal basis for richer main courses.

CLEAR SOUP WITH LEMON AND TOFU

2 pints (1.1 litres) clear stock
4oz (100g) tofu, cut into ½in (1.25cm) cubes
1 small lemon, sliced thinly

Serves 4

Bring the stock to the boil and add the tofu. Reduce the heat and simmer for a few minutes. Divide the soup and tofu between four bowls, taking care not to crush the bean curd.

Decorate each bowl with slices of lemon and leek. Do not crowd the bowls with ingredients. If you have too much lemon or leek, save it for future use.

Substantial soups These three soups are particularly sustaining, as they are packed with nutrients. Avocado soup (bottom left), Javanese vegetable soup (left), and Tuscan haricot bean soup (right) are ideal midday meals.

TUSCAN HARICOT BEAN SOUP

2 tablespoons (30ml) vegetable oil
2 cloves, garlic, crushed
1 medium onion, sliced
1 carrot, chopped
2 stalks celery and leaves, chopped
8oz (225g) tinned plum tomatoes
1 teaspoon (5ml) rosemary, finely chopped
1/4 teaspoon (1.25ml) chilli powder or hot pepper sauce
8oz (225g) haricot beans, soaked overnight, drained
2 pints (1.1litres) water
Salt and black pepper to taste
Parmesan cheese

Serves 4

Heat the oil in a heavy saucepan and sauté the garlic and onion until just softened. Add the carrot and celery and sauté until the onion is browned. Stir in the tomatoes, rosemary and chilli powder. Add the haricot beans and water and bring to the boil. Reduce heat cover and simmer for 1½ to 2 hours. With a slotted spoon remove half the beans and purée in a blender or food processor. Return this purée to the pot, season to taste with a salt and pepper, and return to the boil. Add 1oz (25g) spaghetti, broken into 1in (2.5cm) pieces if you like, and cook until it is al dente and serve garnished with Parmesan cheese.

AVOCADO SOUP

2oz (50g) butter
1in (2.5cm) piece ginger root, peeled and thinly sliced
2oz (50g) flour
1 pint (0.5 litre) milk
Peel of ½ a lemon, grated
2 medium avocados, stoned and skinned
8fl oz (225ml) cream
Salt to taste

Serves 4

Melt the butter in a heavy saucepan and sauté the ginger root over gentle heat for five minutes. Stir in the flour to form a smooth mixture and cook for two to three minutes. Slowly beat in the milk, add the lemon peel and cook the sauce over low heat, stirring, for a 10 minutes.

Remove the sauce from the heat. Leave to cool a little and then blend it with the avocado flesh. Season to taste. Stir in the cream and chill.

JAVANESE VEGETABLE SOUP (SAYUR LODEH)

This is a delicious spicy soup made thick and creamy by the addition of coconut milk. Use a combination of vegetables to your liking, adding them to the pot in the order, that is to say, the one that cooks longest first.

1lb (450g) of a variety of vegetables
2 pints (1 litre) water
1 medium onion, finely diced
2 cloves garlic, crushed
½-1 green or red chilli, finely chopped
2 bay leaves
1 grated lemon rind or chopped lemon grass
1½tsp (7.5ml) ground coriander
1tsp (5ml) dark brown sugar
8fl oz (225 ml) coconut milk Salt and pepper to taste

Prepare the vegetables. Bring the water to the boil in a heavy saucepan. Add the onion, garlic and chilli, bay leaves, lemon rind or lemon grass, coriander and brown sugar. Stir well, cover and leave to simmer for 15 minutes.

Add the vegetables in order of their cooking times, leaving the quick-cooking, leafy ones like watercress or spinach to the very end. After all the vegetables have been added, continue cooking until they are very tender. Add the coconut milk.

Stir in the coconut milk, season to taste with salt and pepper and return the soup to a gentle boil, stirring constantly. Simmer for five minutes and then serve.

To Prepare Coconut Milk from Fresh Coconut

1 fresh small coconut
12fl oz (350ml) water

Grate the flesh of the coconut into a bowl and add the water. Squeeze the flesh in the water for a minute or two to press out all the milk. Strain the liquid off, press the pulp to remove the last residue of juice.

RED BEAN SOUP

2 tablespoons (30ml) vegetable oil
1 clove garlic
1 medium onion, sliced
1 green pepper, deseeded, sliced
2 large tomatoes, chopped
8oz (225g) red kidney beans (or pinto or pink beans) soaked overnight, drained
2 pints (1.1 litres) water
½ teaspoon (1.25ml) hot pepper sauce or chili powder

Serves 4

Heat the oil in a heavy saucepan and add the garlic, onion, and green pepper. Sauté until the onion is golden. Add the tomatoes, beans, water and hot pepper sauce. Stir well and season to taste with salt and black pepper. Bring to the boil, reduce heat, cover and simmer until the beans are soft and tender (about 1 hour).

Remove half the beans with a slotted spoon, purèe, return to the soup, heat through and serve.

Variation

To make a real meal of the soup, add a piece of toasted French bread sprinkled with grated cheese to each bowl.

VEGETABLE MISO SOUP

2 tablespoons (30ml) vegetable oil
2oz (50g) mushrooms, sliced
4oz (100g) daikon (Japanese white radish) cut in matchsticks
1 small onion, diced
4oz (100g) burdock root, peeled and grated (optional)
4oz (100g) miso (fermented soya bean paste)
2 pints (1.1 litres) clear stock or water
2 tablespoons parsley, chopped

Serves 4

Place the oil in a heavy pan, and sauté the mushrooms, daikon, onion and burdock. When the onions are soft add the stock and bring to the boil.

Cream the miso and stir into the soup. Return to the boil, and serve garnished with parsley.

TOMATO AND RICE SOUP

2 tablespoons (30ml) vegetable oil
1 large onion, chopped
1 teaspoon (5ml) dried basil
1 bay leaf
1 tablespoon (15ml) wholemeal flour
1 small carrot, scrubbed and chopped
1 stick celery, chopped
1 teaspoon (5ml) honey or brown sugar
1 tablespoon (15ml) cider vinegar
14oz canned tomatoes, chopped (reserve juice)

1 pint (0.5 litre) water
1 small clove garlic, crushed
Soya sauce to taste
Salt to taste
2fl oz (50ml) soya milk
3 tablespoons (45ml) cooked rice
2 tablespoons (30ml) roasted sunflower seeds to garnish the top

Serves 4-6

Heat the oil in a pan and sauté the onion, basil and bay leaf for five minutes. Stir in the flour. Add the carrot, celery, honey or sugar, cider vinegar, tomatoes with their juice and the water. Bring to the boil, reduce heat, cover and cook for 20 minutes.

Liquidize the soup in a blender with the garlic, soya sauce and salt. Add the soya milk and cooked rice. Reheat and serve with a sprinkling of roasted sunflower seeds.

CUCUMBER AND YOGHURT

1 medium cucumber, peeled and finely chopped
1½pt (850ml) yoghurt
10fl oz (275ml) cold water
2oz (50g) dried fruit, washed, soaked and chopped (optional)
1 tablespoon (15ml) finely chopped fresh mint or parsley
Juice of ½ a lemon
1 clove garlic, finely chopped
Salt and black pepper to taste

Serves 4

Salt the chopped cucumber, reserving a little for decoration, and leave for 30 minutes. Rinse and drain.

Beat the yoghurt and water together together. Add most of the cucumber and the remaining ingredients. Chill well and serve garnished with the reserved cucumber.

FRESH PEA SOUP

2oz (50g) butter
1 medium onion, diced
2 sticks celery, chopped
2 small potatoes, diced
1lb (450g) fresh peas, shelled
1½ (850ml) water or stock
½ teaspoon (2.5ml) English mustard
Pinch ground cloves
1 teaspoon (5ml) dried basil
Salt and black pepper to taste
Parmesan cheese

Serves 4

Melt the butter in a heavy saucepan and sauté the onion for 2 or 3 minutes. Add the celery and potatoes and sautéa further 2 minutes. Add the peas, water or stock, mustard, cloves and basil; stir well. Season to taste with salt and black pepper and bring to the boil. Reduce heat and simmer until the peas and other vegetables are soft and tender (for 10 to 15 minutes).

The soup may be served immediately or blended and reheated before serving. Serve garnished with Parmesan cheese.

CUCUMBERS WITH FETA CHEESE

1 medium cucumber, peeled and diced
1 medium onion, finely diced
6oz (175g) Feta cheese. (If Feta cheese is not available, any crumbly tangy white cheese can be substituted.)
2 tablespoons (30ml) olive oil
Juice of 1 lemon
Salt and black pepper to taste

Serves 4

Combine the cucumber and onion and mix well. Crumble the Feta cheese into a separate bowl. Beat in the oil, lemon juice, and salt and black pepper to taste. Pour the mixture over the cucumber and onion and serve.

AVOCADO AND LEMON DIP

The sweet flesh of the avocado perfectly partners the sour lemon juice. Serve this dip immediately after you have made it, or it will begin to discolour. If you really want to leave it for a while, put the avocado stones back into the dip and cover tightly with cling film.

2 medium-sized ripe avocados, stoned and skinned
Juice and grated rind of 1 lemon
2 cloves garlic, crushed
Salt and black pepper to taste
Up to ¼pt (150ml) vegetable oil (olive oil is best)

Serves 4-6

Put the avocado flesh, lemon rind, lemon juice and garlic into a blender or food processor (or mix by hand) and make a smooth paste; add salt and black pepper to taste.

With the blender at the slowest speed, slowly add the oil. Stop when the mixture no longer absorbs the oil easily, or when the taste is to your liking.

GREEN BEANS IN OIL

1 lb (450g) fresh or frozen green beans (string beans)
3 tablespoons (45ml) olive oil
1 medium onion, finely sliced
3 large tomatoes
2 cloves garlic, crushed
½ teaspoon (2.5ml) sugar
Salt and black pepper to taste
Water
Juice of 1 lemon

Either defrost the beans or, if fresh, wash them well, top and tail, and where necessary string them. Cut the beans in half, or, if they are very long, cut them into 2in (5cm) lengths.

Sauté the onion in the oil in a heavy pan until it is just soft, then add the tomatoes and cook until they are soft. Add the beans and stir well. Add the garlic and sugar and season to taste with salt and black pepper. Just cover the

Summertime suppers Serve cucumbers and feta cheese with fried tofu and black olives for this delicious, light summer starter.

contents of the pan with water and simmer for 30 minutes or until the beans are very tender. Leave them to cool in the pan until lukewarm or cold. Just before serving squeeze the lemon juice over the beans.

FRIED CHEESE WITH OLIVES

Hot, fried cubes of cheese served with a light sprinkling of lemon juice are delicious. Greek cheeses such as Haloumi, Kephalotyri and Kasseri (found in Greek stores) are ideal for this, but hard Cheddar or Gruyere can make good substitutes. In this Egyptian recipe the cheese is fried in butter with olives. Serve with fresh bread and slices of lemon.

1 tablespoon (15ml) butter
8oz (225g) firm or hard cheese cut into ½in (1.25cm) cubes
10-15 black olives, halved and pitted

Melt the butter in a small, heavy frying pan and add the cheese and olives. Fry gently, turning the cheese cubes frequently until they are very hot all the way through. Serve immediately.

CHICK PEA AND YOGHURT DIP

8oz (225g) chick peas, tinned or cooked soft
4fl oz (100ml) yoghurt
Juice of 1 lemon
1 teaspoon crushed dried mint
Salt and black pepper to taste
Rind of ½ a lemon, grated

Blend together the first four ingredients. Season the mixture to taste with salt and black pepper, and thin down with water if it's too thick. Serve garnished with grated lemon peel. Diced green pepper and/or celery added to the dip after it has been made gives it a pleasant crunchy texture.

SAVOURY PEANUT FRITTERS

These fritters can be served as a snack with drinks or as an accompaniment to rice and curries.

1 small onion, grated
1 clove garlic, crushed
2 teaspoons (10ml) ground coriander
½ teaspoon (2.5ml) ground cumin
½ teaspoon (2.5 ml) ground turmeric
5oz (150g) rice flour
8fl oz (225ml) water or coconut milk
Salt to taste
6oz (175g) roasted peanuts
Vegetable oil for shallow frying

Serves 4

Put the onion, garlic, coriander, cumin, turmeric, flour and water or coconut milk into a blender and blend to a smooth batter. Transfer the batter to a bowl and add salt to taste. Stir the peanuts into the batter.

Heat 2 tablespoons (30ml) of oil in a shallow frying pan, drop in 3-4 tablespoon (45-60ml) amounts of peanut batter and spread it evenly by tilting the pan back and forth. The batter does not need to cover the whole surface of the pan. Fry until brown and crisp on the underside. Turn over and brown the other side. Drain on absorbent paper draped over a wire rack. Repeat for all the batter. Serve hot or store in an airtight container.

BUTTERBEAN AND OLIVE STARTER

This is a tasty, simple, colourful and healthy starter.

4oz (100g) black olives, stoned and chopped
2oz (50g) carrots, scrubbed and finely grated
4oz (100g) butterbeans, soaked and cooked or 8oz (225g) tinned butterbeans, drained
2 teaspoons (10ml) dried oregano
1 teaspoon (5ml) white wine
1oz (25g) roasted cashew nuts
Chopped parsley to garnish

Serves 4

Mix the olives and carrot with the butterbeans. Stir in the oregano, wine and nuts. Serve cold garnished with parsley.

ASPARAGUS AND CUCUMBER SALAD

This salad may also be prepared with French beans, broccoli, Brussels sprouts. Lightly stir-fried bean sprouts or bamboo shoots as a substitute for asparagus.

- 2 tablespoons (30ml) vegetable oil
- 2 tablespoons (30ml) sesame seeds
- 3 tablespoons (45ml) vinegar
- 3 tablespoons (45ml) sugar
- 1 teaspoon (5ml) soy sauce
- ½ teaspoon black pepper
- 12oz (350g) asparagus
- ½ medium cucumber

Heat the oil in a frying pan, and fry the sesame seeds until brown. Remove the seeds, cool and stir them into the vinegar, sugar, soy sauce and pepper. Remove the base and tough stringy part of the asparagus, then cut them into 1 inch (2.5cm) long pieces. Parboil in a little salted water for four to five minutes. Drain. Cut cucumber in half lengthwise and then into 3-inch (7.5cm) long matchsticks. Combine cucumber and asparagus, pour over sauce, and carefully mix in. Chill for 30 minutes. Serve.

Subtle flavours The unmistakeably delicate flavour of asparagus is delicious when combined with the freshness of cucumber.

CHICK PEA AND TAHINI DIP

8oz (225g) chick peas washed, drained, covered with water and soaked overnight; or use 396g (14oz) tinned chick peas and ignore the first paragraph of the recipe
2pt (1.1l) water
Juice of 2 lemons
5fl oz (150ml) tahini
3 cloves crushed garlic
Salt to taste

For the garnish
Olive oil
Paprika
Chopped parsley
Reserved chick peas

Serves 4-6

Drain the soaked chick peas and place them in a heavy pot with the fresh water. Bring them to the boil and remove any foam that forms. Gently boil the peas for 1½ hours or until they easily crush between thumb and forefinger. Drain the peas and reserve any cooking liquid. Put aside one tablespoon (15ml) of peas for garnishing.

Put the cooked peas, lemon juice, tahini and garlic into a blender or food processor with enough cooking liquid (and plain water, if needed) to allow the mixture to puree satisfactorily. Add salt to taste and, if needed, more lemon juice or tahini to taste. Blend again, and serve.

Spoon the prepared humus onto a serving dish, sprinkle with paprika and chopped parsley and pour 1-2 tablespoons (15-30ml) of olive oil over it. Finally, garnish with the reserved cooked chick peas. Serve with warm pitta bread.

FALAFEL

1lb (450g) chick peas, soaked for 24 hours, drained
3 cloves garlic
2 teaspoons (10ml) ground coriander
2 teaspoons (10ml) ground cumin
1 teaspoon (5ml) baking powder
2 tablespoons (30ml) chopped parsley
Salt and black pepper to taste
Oil for shallow frying

Serves 4-6

Put a quarter of the chick peas into a blender or food processor with the garlic, coriander, cumin, baking powder and parsley. Liquidize and keep adding a few more chick peas and then blending until they are all in. You will need to add some water to get them to purée but use as little as possible. Season with salt and transfer to a bowl. Leave the mixture to rest for 30 minutes. Form dessertspoonsful of the mixture into round balls.

Heat the oil in a frying pan and fry the falafel for 2-3 minutes or until golden brown and crisp. Drain well and serve hot or cold.

AUBERGINE HORS D'OEUVRE

2 medium aubergines
2fl oz (50ml) vegetable oil
8fl oz (225ml) yoghurt
Salt and pepper to taste

Serves 4

Peel the aubergines and cut them into ½in (1.25cm) thick slices. Put the slices in a colander and generously salt them. Set aside for 30 minutes. Now wash and drain them and pat them dry.

Fry the aubergine slices in the oil in a heavy frying pan until well cooked and brown on both sides. Season the yoghurt and pour half into a bowl. Arrange the aubergine slices on top and pour over them the remaining yoghurt. Chill and serve. Garnish with a little parsley or mint.

SPICED AUBERGINE DIP

2 medium aubergines or 1 large, washed, dried
2 tablespoons (30ml) olive oil
2 or more cloves garlic
salt and cayenne or chili sauce

Serves 4-6

Preheat the oven to 350°F (175°C, gas mark 4). Rub the aubergines with a little oil and place them on a tray in the oven on a middle shelf. Bake them for 45 minutes or until the interiors are soft and well done. Peel the skin off them as soon as they are cool enough to touch.

Put the flesh in a bowl or blender, add the garlic and oil and beat them into a puree. Add salt and cayenne or chili sauce to taste. Chill and serve.

MUSHROOM PATE

2 tablespoons (30ml) vegetable oil
1 large onion, chopped
2 teaspoons (10ml) chopped fresh rosemary or 1 teaspoon dried rosemary
1 small clove garlic, crushed
12 oz (350 g) mushrooms, washed and chopped
2 tablespoons (30ml) wholemeal flour
1 tablespoon (15ml) soya flour
1 teaspoon (5ml) miso soya sauce to taste

Heat the oil in a pan and sauté the onion, rosemary and garlic for about five minutes. Add the mushrooms and cook over a moderate heat for five minutes. Add the flour and sŏya flour and cook, stirring, for 10 minutes.

Put the mixture into a blender or food processor and add the soya sauce and miso. Blend the mixture to a smooth paste and serve.

Greek delights Olives marinated in lemon and coriander and dolmas (stuffed vine leaves) form the centrepieces of this attractive arrangement of mezze. All these dishes originated in Greece; they make extremely attractive starters and dips or the perfect constituents of an al fresco picnic.

CRUDITES WITH AIOLI

Aioli is a garlic-flavoured mayonnaise. It originated in southern France, but is said to be derived from a recipe for the Spanish sauce ali-oli. Aioli can be served with a variety of ingredients, including eggs, and is delicious with fresh raw vegetables (crudités). The vegetables are cleaned, neatly cut up, lightly chilled and then served in a central bowl, with separate bowls of the aioli dip.

4 beetroots, sliced
8 sticks celery, washed, cut in half
6 medium carrots, peeled and cut lengthwise into sticks
1 medium cucumber, cut into 3in (7.5cm) lengths and quartered
6 tomatoes, quartered
2 green peppers, deseeded and sliced

For the aioli:
6-8 medium cloves garlic salt
2 egg yolks
9fl oz (250ml) olive oil
White pepper to taste
Juice of 2 medium lemons

Prepare the vegetables and arrange them attractively on a serving dish. Put them in the refrigerator to chill for about an hour. Make the aioli. Crush the garlic with a little salt. Beat the egg yolks in a bowl and stir in the garlic paste. Add the oil, drop by drop, beating all the time, until the sauce thickens. Then add the oil a little faster until it has all been used up. Season to taste with salt and pepper and stir in the lemon juice. Alternatively, put the garlic, egg yolks and, a little salt in a food blender or processor and add the oil slowly to form a thick sauce. Season to taste with salt and pepper and add the lemon juice.

A feast of colours Crudités with aioli is an ideal dish to serve as a starter for an informal meal, or as a tasty party hors d'oeuvre.

DOLMAS

Dolmas is a general name for stuffed vegetables although, as far as mezze are concerned, the name usually refers to stuffed vine or cabbage leaves (and less often to Swiss chard). The stuffing is usually rice and vegetables.

STUFFED VINE LEAVES

8oz (225g) tinned or packeted vine leaves or 340 fresh leaves

For the filling:
1lb (450g) cooked long grain rice
1 medium onion, finely diced
1½ tablespoons (17.5ml) currants (optional)
2 tablespoons (30ml) tomato purée
2 cloves garlic, crushed
2 tablespoons (30ml) finely chopped mint or parsley
1 teaspoon (5ml) ground cinnamon
Salt and black pepper to taste
Boiling water
Juice of 2 lemons
1 tablespoon (15ml) olive oil or other vegetable oil
Water or vegetable stock
Lemon slices
Sprigs of fresh mint or parsley

Put the tinned, packeted or fresh leaves in a large bowl and scald them with the boiling water. Leave them to soak for a few minutes to disentangle themselves. Now drain them and rinse with cold water. Separate the leaves as you stuff them or better still separate them first and leave them to drain on absorbent paper, dull side up.

Make the filling. Combine all the ingredients in a large bowl and mix well.

Layer the bottom of a heavy pan or casserole with broken leaves, or about 10 full leaves in all.

To stuff the vine leaves, take one leaf at a time, cut off the stem if it has one and place about 1 tablespoon (15ml) of filling in the centre. Fold the stem end of the leaf over the filling. Fold in the sides and roll up carefully from the stem end to form a nice firm packet about 2in (5cm) long. Layer the stuffed leaves into the pan, side by side, seam side down. Sprinkle them with the lemon juice and olive oil and add enough water or stock to just cover the dolmas. Place an inverted plate or saucer over the dolmas to hold them down. Cover the pot and simmer for 1 hour. Make sure the dolmas stay moist during cooking.

Leave them to cool in the pot if you are serving them cold. Drain and arrange on a serving tray in neat straight lines and then garnish.

MARINATED OLIVES

Ideally, the olives should be marinated for at least a week for the full flavour of the lemon and coriander to be absorbed, so this part of the mezze table needs advance planning. This recipe calls for a good quantity of olives and you may not need this many all at once. They will keep for a long time, however, and will still be delicious at a later date.

2lb (900g) black or green olives or mixed, drained if in brine
2 tablespoons (30ml) coriander seeds
2 small lemons, thinly sliced
Olive oil
Sprigs of parsley for garnish

Serves 4-6

Pick over the olives and discard any bruised ones. With a thin sharp knife cut two or three shallow slits into each. Wash them well under running cold water and drain. Prepare two clean pickling jars. Put the olives into a bowl and combine them with the coriander seeds.

Pack the mixture into the jars, adding slices of lemon evenly throughout the jar as you proceed. Pour olive oil slowly into each jar until it reaches the brim. Seal the jars with the lids and store in a cool place for at least a week before serving. Serve garnished with sprigs of parsley.

There is nothing to beat making your own bread and pastries, using good wholemeal flour and other unrefined ingredients. Pitta bread is particularly versatile, as it can be dipped in purèes of beans and sauces or stuffed with salads, vegetables or vegetable burgers.

CROISSANTS

Croissants are delicious but they contain far too much fat to be considered a regular part of a healthy diet so save them for a special celebration breakfast. These croissants will deep freeze successfully, either baked or unbaked.

½oz (15g) fresh yeast or 1½ teaspoons (7.5ml) dried yeast
1oz (25g) sugar
about 7fl oz (200ml) soya milk diluted with 7fl oz (200ml) water
1lb 2oz (500g) wholemeal flour
2 teaspoons (10ml) salt
8oz (225g) hard vegetable margarine, cut in small pieces

Dissolve the yeast and sugar in 12fl oz (350ml) of the soya milk solution and mix in 6oz (175g) flour. Add the rest of the flour and salt and mix to a dough. Rest the dough, covered, for 30 minutes then roll it out ½in (1cm) thick into a rectangle twice as long as wide.

Dot half the surface with all the margarine and fold the other half on top. Roll this out then refold and roll out again. Repeat twice more, turning the dough through 45 degrees each time. Rest the dough for 15 minutes.

Roll it out into a sheet ⅛in (2.5mm) thick. Cut the dough into strips 8in (20cm) wide. Cut the strips into triangles of 6in (15cm) base and 4in (10cm) sides and roll these up into a croissant shape, starting with the long side.

Place the croissants on a warmed, greased baking tray and brush them with soya milk solution. Prove them for about 30 minutes, covered, in a warm place, then brush them again with the soya milk solution.

Preheat the oven to 425°F (220°C) gas mark 7. Bake the croissants in the hot oven for 20 minutes. Remove and allow to cool.

CHAPATTIS

8oz (225g) 100% wholewheat flour
2 tablespoons (30ml) vegetable oil
½ teaspoon (2.5ml) salt
water (about 6fl oz/175ml)

Makes 8

Mix the flour, oil, salt and water in a bowl to form a fairly stiff dough that comes away from the side of the bowl.

Breakfast treats Fresh homemade breads make a tasty start to the day. Croissants (right) are a firm, though fattening, favourite, as are oatcakes (left), and yeasted bread rolls (top).

Knead the dough until the texture is smooth and elastic.

Pinch off 8 pieces and roll them into balls. Flatten the balls on a floured board roll them out thinly into circles approximately 8in (20cm) in diameter.

Heat a heavy ungreased frying pan over a high flame. Place a chapatti in it, cook the chapatti for about 1 minute and then turn it over. Press the edges with a spatula; they should puff up slightly. Continue cooking until the underside is just mottled with brown spots.

Remove the chapatti from the pan and store it in a heated oven or wrap in a clean cloth to keep it warm while you cook the others.

OATCAKES

8oz (225g) medium oatmeal
2oz (50g) wholemeal flour
1 teaspoon (5ml) baking powder
2oz (50g) soft vegetable margarine
boiling water to mix

Makes about 20

Preheat oven to 375°F (190°C) gas mark 5. Mix together the oatmeal, flour and baking powder. Rub in the margarine and add just enough boiling water to form a firm dough. Knead the dough well and roll it out to ⅛in (3mm) thick.

Cut the oatcakes out with a plain 2½in (6cm) cutter. Place them on a greased baking tray and bake for 10 minutes in the preheated oven.

Remove the tray from the oven, transfer the biscuits to a wire grill and cool. Store unused oatcakes in an airtight container.

BASIC WHOLEMEAL BREAD

This bread keeps well, and it can be used up to one week after baking. All wholemeal flours do not bake in the same way, so do experiment with different brands of flour (and with the given recipe) until the bread you make is exactly to your liking.

2 teaspoons (10ml) brown sugar
¾oz (20g) fresh yeast or 1 level tablespoon active dried yeast
¾ pint (425ml) slightly warm water
1½ (700g) wholemeal flour
1 tablespoon (15ml) salt
1 tablespoon (15ml) vegetable oil
cracked wheat or sesame seeds (optional)
1 tablespoon (15ml) melted butter

Makes 2 two lb (450g) loaves

Mix the sugar, yeast and a little of the water into a smooth paste in a small bowl and set it aside in a warm place for 15 minutes or until the mixture has frothed up. Sift the flour and salt into a large mixing bowl and add the yeast mixture, oil and remaining water.

Knead the mixture until you have a smooth springy dough that comes away from the sides of the bowl. Turn the dough onto a floured board and knead well for about 5 minutes (longer if you have strong arms).

Wash, dry and slightly grease the mixing bowl, place the dough in it, cover the bowl with a warm damp cloth and set it aside in a warm place for 1 to 1½ hours or until the dough has risen to double its original size.

Knead the dough again for 5 minutes and then divide it into 2 equal parts. Shape the dough pieces and place them into two lightly buttered 1lb (450g) bread tins. Sprinkle the cracked wheat or sesame seeds on to the top of each loaf, cover the tins with a warm, damp cloth and leave them in a warm place for 30 to 45 minutes, or until the dough has risen to the top of the tins.

Preheat the oven to 450°F (230°C) gas mark 8, place the tins in the centre of the oven and bake for 40 minutes. Remove the bread from the oven, tip the loaves out of the tins and knock the underside. If the bread sounds hollow it is cooked. If the bread does not sound hollow, return the loaves, upside down, to the oven and bake for a further 10

minutes at 375°F (190°C, gas mark 5. Leave the bread to cool on a wire rack, or resting across the top of the empty bread tins.

WHOLEMEAL FRENCH BREAD

4fl oz (100ml) warm water
4fl oz (100ml) warm milk
4fl oz (100ml) natural yoghurt
¾oz (20g) fresh yeast or 1 level tablespoon active dried yeast
1 tablespoon (15ml) sugar
1 teaspoon (5ml) salt
1 tablespoon (10ml) melted butter
1½lb (700g) wholemeal flour

Makes two 1lb (450g) loaves

Combine the water, milk, yoghurt, yeast and sugar in a mixing bowl. Stir well and leave in a warm place for 15 minutes or until the mixture is frothy. Add the remaining flour and mix it in.

Knead the dough in the bowl until it has lost any stickiness and then turn it out onto a floured board and knead it for a further 5 to 10 minutes. The finished dough should be firm and quite stiff; add a little more flour if it is not.

Wash, dry and lightly grease the mixing bowl. Put the dough back in, cover with a clean cloth and leave it to rise for 1 hour or until doubled in size. Punch the dough down and divide it in half. Roll each portion out into a large square (about 12in (30cm) across) on a floured board. Fold two opposite sides of a square into the middle, then fold this in half lengthways. Press all the edges together so that no seams are visible. Repeat for the other square. Lightly butter two baking sheets and place a loaf on each, cover it with a clean cloth and leave to rise in a warm place for 1½ hours or until doubled in size.

Preheat the oven to 425°F (220°C) gas mark 7. Make four or five diagonal cuts about about ½in (1cm) deep in the top of each loaf and then lightly brush each with a little cold water (to give a crunchy texture to the crust). Put the loaves in the middle or the lower middle of the oven and bake for 30 to 35 minutes (longer if the loaves are thick rather than long). After 15 minutes baking, brush the loaves once more with a little water.

WHOLEMEAL PITTA BREAD

Pitta bread, a staple food of the Middle East, it is round and flat with a hollow in the middle. The texture is soft, even on the outside and it is delicious for eating with dips such as humus or for mopping up sauces.

½oz (12.5g) fresh yeast or 1 level teaspoon active dried yeast
2fl oz (50ml) warm water
1 teaspoon (5ml) sugar
1lb (450g) wholemeal flour
½ teaspoon (1.5ml) salt
10fl oz (275ml) water

Makes 15 pitta breads

Mix the yeast, warm water and sugar into a smooth paste in a small bowl and set it aside in a warm place for 15 minutes or until the mixture has frothed up. Sift the flour and salt into a mixing bowl and pour in the yeast mixture.

Knead by hand and slowly add the water to form a firm dough, neither too hard nor too soft. Turn the dough onto a floured board and knead it for 10 to 15 minutes. This is vital if the bread is to have the right texture.

Lightly grease a large bowl, place the dough in it and leave it in a warm place for 1½ to 2 hours or until doubled in size.

Knead the dough again for 2 to 3 minutes then divide it into 15 equal portions.

Form them into balls and roll them into circles ¼in (0.5cm) thick on a floured board. Dust each round with flour and set to rise again on a floured cloth in a warm place for about 20 minutes.

Meanwhile preheat the oven to 450°F (230°C) gas mark 8. After 10 minutes place 2 ungreased baking sheets in the oven to warm up. Lightly sprinkle the dough rounds with cold water and put them on the hot baking sheets.

Place them in the oven and bake for about 8 minutes. Do not open the oven door during this time. The finished pitta bread should be soft and white with a hollow in the middle.

Variations on a theme Bread comes in a surprising variety of textures and tastes. The firmer crunchy types, such as sourdough bread (right), are as popular as the softer breads, such as Armenian round bread (left). Satisfy all tastes by baking batches of both sorts.

ARMENIAN ROUND BREAD

1¼lb (575g) plain flour
1 teaspoon (5ml) salt
1oz (25g) fresh yeast, or 2 teaspoons (10ml) dried yeast
2 teaspoons (5ml) sugar
4fl oz ((100ml) warm water
8fl oz (225ml) warm milk
2oz (50g) melted butter

Makes 2 loaves

Mix the salt and flour in a bowl and make a well in the centre. Dissolve the sugar and crumble in the yeast. Pour this, the warm milk and half the butter, melted, into the flour well.

Knead the dough again for another few minutes and then set it aside, covered, for another hour. Now divide the dough in half and form each half into a ball shape. Roll each ball into a disc about 1in (2.5cm) thick and 8 to 9in (20 to 22.5cm) in diameter.

Grease 2 baking trays and place a round of dough on each. Brush the tops with the remaining melted butter and set aside, covered, for a further hour.

Preheat the oven to 375°F (190°C) gas mark 5. Bake the bread on the middle sheet for about 45 minutes or until it is firm and nicely browned.

SOURDOUGH BREAD

This is a quick and easy sourdough method using wheat and rye flours.

1lb (450g) rye flour
1½lb (700g) strong wholewheat flour
¾oz (20g) salt
1 pint (0.5 litre) warm water
¾oz (20g) fresh yeast or 2 teaspoons (10ml) dried yeast
2 tablespoons (30ml) caraway seeds

Makes 3 long loaves

Weigh half the flours and salt into a bowl, mix well and then mix in half the warm water. Leave this to stand, covered, for 12-16 hours or until it smells slightly sour.

Combine this mixture with the rest of the flours, salt, yeast and water. Mix well and knead for 5 minutes. Cover the bowl with a damp cloth and set aside in a warm place for 1½ hours. Knock it back and, whilst doing so, knead in the caraway seeds. Shape the dough into loaves.

Place the loaves on greased baking trays and prove for another hour, covered and in a warm place.

Preheat the oven to 400°F (200°C) gas mark 6. Bake the bread in the hot oven for 1 hour. If the bread starts to brown too much at this temperature reduce it accordingly. Once baked, remove and cool on a wire rack.

SALADS

Salads are one of the cornerstones of a vegetarian meal. Raw vegetables and fruit contain all their original nutrients and fibre, since they loose none through cooking or processing.

When possible, buy vegetables grown locally and in season. In this way you will get them at their freshest and cheapest. If you can obtain organically-grown vegetables readily, they are really worth buying, since their flavour is better and they are free from pesticides.

DRESSING SALADS

For most salads it is wise to use a minimum quantity of dressing. This is for two reasons. Firstly the aim is to complement the taste, not submerge it. Secondly, dressings usually contain oils and creams and though we would not do without them, these fat-rich ingredients should be used in moderation.

Always taste dressings before pouring them over the vegetables and adjust them to your personal preference. Another reason for tasting is that many ingredients are of variable strength, sweetness and flavour – tomatoes, carrots, oranges, chillies, paprika, vinegars and above all, shoyu sauce are all unpredictable, so you should test each new ingredient in advance.

DRESSING LEAF SALADS

It is worth reserving your very best olive oil for your leaf salads. Curly endive and dandelion are best dressed with walnut oil, but use it on other leaf salads as well if you like its flavour.

Make your dressing with a 4/1 oil/vinegar ration, or if you are using delicate leaves a 5/1 ratio.

Never dress your leaf salads until the very last moment, preferably at the table.

Toss your salad gently but thoroughly scooping the leaves from the bottom of the heap to the top several times over.

SUMMER GREEN LEAF SALAD

Assorted summer green leaves
Vinaigrette dressing
made with olive or walnut oil (4-5 parts oil to 1 part lemon)
Hyssop, nasturtium, borage or chive flowers

Carefully wash the summer green leaves under cold running water. Gently tear up the larger leaves.

Dress and toss them just before serving with the vinaigrette.

Garnish the salad with the flowers and serve at once.

PEAR, GRAPE AND CUCUMBER SALAD

A simple, yet unusual combination, which makes a good side salad for a dish with cheese in it or simply as an accompaniment to cheese and bread. Served well chilled, it also makes an appetizing starter.

3 ripe but firm sweet pears peeled and cored, one pear thinly sliced, the rest diced
½ medium cucumber, divided in half lengthwise, seeds scooped out (slice ¼ cucumber, dice the rest)
4oz (100g) black or green seedless grapes, washed
vinaigrette dressing

Serves 4-6

Make a bed of the pear and cucumber slices in a small salad bowl. Put the remaining pear, cucumber and grapes (reserve 5 or 6 grapes) into a bowl and toss them in vinaigrette dressing to taste.

Pour this mixture over the bed of pear and cucumber slices. Garnish with grapes, chill and serve.

WATERCRESS AND PEAR SALAD

½ bunch watercress, washed, drained
1 medium-sized ripe pear, quartered and cut across into 0.5cm (¾in) slices
1 head of chicory, leaves separated and washed
2 teaspoons (10ml) Olive oil
Black pepper to taste
2oz (50g) blue stilton (optional)

Serves 4

Combine the watercress, pear and chicory leaves in a mixing bowl. Pour in the oil and grind in about 4 twists of black pepper from the mill. Toss the salad until pear juices begin to run. Serve the salad on individual side plates and if you wish, crumble over each a little Stilton.

GREEN SALAD WITH COCONUT SAUCE

Prepare a green salad from a selection of vegetables in season, for example, lettuce, cabbage, Chinese cabbage, watercress, spinach (lightly cooked), French or green beans (sliced and parboiled), young peas in their pods. Make the coconut sauce by combining dessicated coconut with hot water, onion, chilli powder, garlic and lemon juice to taste and toss the salad in it.

TABBOULEH

Tabbouleh is a beautiful bright green and nutritious salad in which the major ingredient is bulgar or burghul wheat. It has a sharp, refreshing flavour and is perfect for a hot summer day. In its simplest form it is served in individual lettuce-lined bowls or stuffed into pitta bread. However, the best way to serve it is piled high on a large dish and garnished with cucumber, tomatoes and olives.

8oz (225g) bulgar or burghul wheat, coarse grain
1 medium onion, finely diced
2oz (50g) parsley, finely chopped
Salt and black pepper to taste
1oz (25g) fresh mint, finely chopped or 2 tablespoons (30ml) dried mint, crushed
4 tablespoons (60ml) lemon juice
4 tablespoons (60ml) vegetable oil (olive oil if possible)
4oz (100g) tomatoes, thinly sliced
Cucumber, thinly sliced
2oz (50g) olives

Serves 4

Cover the bulgar in water, leave it to soak for 30 minutes to 1 hour. Drain and squeeze out any excess water.

Thoroughly mix the bulgar and onion, stir in the parsley and season to taste with salt and freshly-milled black pepper. Mix the mint, lemon juice and oil together and pour the mixture over the bulgar. Carefully stir it in and finally adjust the taste to suit, with the addition of more seasoning or lemon juice; it should taste quite tangy.

Pile the wheat on a serving dish and decorate with tomatoes, cucumber and olives, and serve.

TURKISH ORANGE AND ONION SALAD

2 large, sweet oranges
2 medium onions, thinly sliced
Black olives, halved and stoned
3 tablespoons (45ml) olive oil or other vegetable oil
Juice of 1 lemon

Peel the oranges, being careful to remove all the white pith, and slice them crosswise into rings.

In a bowl arrange alternate layers of onion and orange. Garnish the top with olives. Combine the olive oil and lemon juice and pour over.

Variation

You can prepare Israeli Orange and Avocad salad in the same way as above, but substitute cubes of avocado flesh for the onions in the original recipe and cut the orange slices into small pieces.

Tangy salads These three salads – Tabbouleh (left), Greek salad (right), and Turkish orange and onion salad (bottom right) – are particularly refreshing and are perfect to enjoy in hotter weather.

GREEK SALAD

1 small lettuce, leaves torn into bite-sized pieces
4oz (100g) feta cheese, cut into small pieces
2oz (50g) black olives
1 firm tomato, chopped
1 tablespoon (15ml) finely diced mild onion
¼ cucumber, sliced
3 tablespoons (45ml) olive oil
Juice of 1 lemon
½ teaspoon (2.5ml) dried oregano.
Salt and pepper to taste

Serves 4

Put torn lettuce leaves into a serving bowl. Add the cheese, olives, tomato, onion and cucumber, pour over the olive oil and lemon juice and season to taste with salt and black pepper. Toss well and serve sprinkled with the herbs.

INDONESIAN FRUIT SALAD (RUJAK)

In this unusual fruit salad, fruits and vegetables are combined and served with a dressing made with chillies, vinegar and plenty of brown sugar. Use any combination of fresh fruit or vegetables in season. A selection is given below. Serve the salad on its own or as part of a larger meal alongside savoury dishes, or as the last course of a lunch.

2 green dessert apples, peeled and cut into pieces
2 oranges, peeled, segmented
1 grapefruit, peeled, segmented
½ fresh pineapple, peeled and cubed or 1 small tin pineapple
1-2 firm mangoes, peeled and cut into pieces
½ cucumber, sliced
1 bunch radishes, washed, topped and tailed

Winter salads Brighten up your winter table with these decorative salads. The clear greens of the apple and spinach salad (left) hint at its unusually fresh flavour, while the exotic colours and taste of the Indonesian rice salad (right), drive wintery gloom away.

Dressing
1 fresh or dried red chilli, seeds removed, finely chopped
1 tablespoon (15ml) dark soya sauce
4oz (100g) dark brown sugar
2 tablespoons (30ml) white vinegar or 2 tablespoons (30ml) lemon juice

Serves 4

Combine all the fruits and vegetables in a large bowl. Mix together all the dressing ingredients and pour the dressing over the fruit salad. Mix well and serve. The dressing can also be served in individual bowls into which each fruit is dipped before eating.

SPINACH AND APPLE SALAD WITH LIME

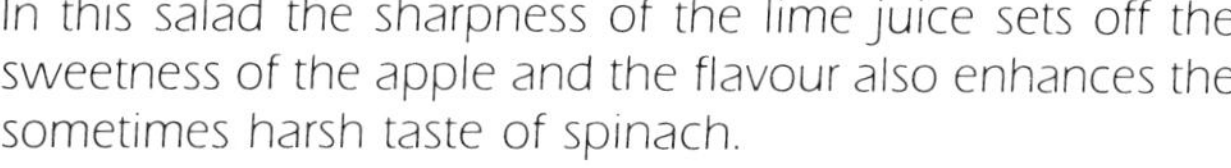

In this salad the sharpness of the lime juice sets off the sweetness of the apple and the flavour also enhances the sometimes harsh taste of spinach.

1lb (450g) fresh spinach, washed and drained
2 medium eating apples, chilled, cored, quartered and chopped into small pieces
2 tablespoons (30ml) vegetable oil
1 tablespoon (15ml) lime juice
Salt and black pepper to taste
Serves 4

Remove any thick spinach stalks; finely shred the leaves. Combine the oil and lime juice and whisk well together.

Mix the spinach and the chilled apples, pour the dressing over this mixture, add salt and black pepper and toss well.

MEXICAN RED BEAN SALAD

A filling salad (or a meal in itself for 4 people if served with bread).

4 tablespoons (60ml) vegetable oil
2 tablespoons (30ml) wine or cider vinegar
8oz (225g) cooked red kidney beans (drained weight)
Salt and black pepper to taste
1 small onion, diced small
1 medium green pepper, seeded, cored and chopped
1 medium avocado, peeled and cubed (optional)
2oz (50g) black olives
1 small lettuce
4oz (100g) grated cheese

Combine the oil, vinegar and red beans and season to taste with salt and black pepper. Mix well and chill in the refrigerator for 30 minutes.

Stir in the onion, green pepper, avocado and olives. Make a bed of torn lettuce leaves in a serving bowl and arrange the bean mixture on top. Sprinkle with cheese.

CHINESE GREENS WITH PEANUT DRESSING

This salad is very good with Chinese flowering cabbage (choi-sum) or if that is unavailable, the same dressing is good with Chinese white cabbage (baak-choi).

8oz (225g) chinese greens (choi-sum), washed, trimmed if necessary, tied into bundles
Salt
2 tablespoons (30ml) creamy peanut butter
1 tablespoon (15ml) shoyu (natural soy sauce)

Drop the bundles of greens into a pan of lightly salted, slowly boiling water for 2 minutes. Drain the greens, separate them from the bundles and immediately rinse them under cold water until cooled.

Chop the greens into 1in (2.5cm) lengths. Mix together the peanut butter and soy sauce (add a little oil if the mixture is too thick). Toss the greens in this dressing and serve them in individual deep serving bowls.

APPLE AND GRAPES WITH MUSTARD SAUCE

This salad also makes an unusual appetizing, bitter-sweet starter.

8oz (225g) eating apples, cored, cut into small chunks
Juice of ½ lemon
8oz (225g) large grapes, washed
2 tablespoons (30ml) Japanese mustard dressing
1 teaspoon (5ml) mustard seeds

Serves 4

Sprinkle the apple with lemon juice and set aside to chill.

Cut the grapes in half and pick out the seeds with the tip of a pointed knife. Lightly chill the grapes.

Toss the apple and grapes in the dressing and garnish with the mustard seeds. Serve in bowls.

VEGETABLE AND TOFU SALAD

Tofu or bean-curd is a soya bean product. It is soft and white with a custard-like texture which easily absorbs the flavours of other ingredients.

2 tablespoons (30ml) sesame oil
3 tablespoons (45ml) shoyu (natural soy sauce)
3 tablespoons (45ml) cider vinegar
1 tablespoon (15ml) water
1 teaspoon (5ml) clear honey
1 clove garlic, crushed
2 blocks 12oz (300g) tofu (bean-curd), cut into 2.5cm (1in) cubes
2 stalks celery, finely chopped
2oz (50g) mushrooms, washed and sliced
4oz (100g) chinese or white cabbage, finely shredded

Serves 4-6

Combine the oil, shoyu, vinegar, water, honey and garlic and mix well together. Put two-thirds of this mixture into a large shallow bowl or containter and add the tofu cubes. Leave them to marinate in the refrigerator for 1 hour.

Transfer the tofu and marinade to a serving bowl and gently stir in the celery, mushrooms and cabbage. Add the remaining dressing, carefully toss the salad and serve.

Eastern flavour Vegetable and tofu salad (left), Chinese greens with peanut dressing (right), and apples and grapes with mustard dressing (bottom), are the perfect complement to Oriental main dishes, but stand on their own as interesting starters too.

TOMATO AND GREEN BEAN SALAD

Sometimes in the winter and spring tomatoes are not very tasty, so here a strongly flavoured yoghurt and tahini dressing is used to compensate for this.

8oz (225g) green beans, fresh or frozen, topped and tailed
1lb (450g) firm tomatoes, quartered
2 tablespoons (30ml) freshly chopped parsley
5oz (125g) natural yoghurt
1 tablespoon (15ml) tahini
1 tablespoon (15ml) lemon juice
½ clove garlic, crushed
Salt and black pepper to taste

Cook the green beans in rapidly boiling salted water for about 7 or 8 minutes or until al dente or firm to the bite. (If using frozen beans, cook according to the instructions on the packet). Cool them rapidly under cold running water to retain the colour and texture. Mix the beans with the tomatoes and most of the parsley (reserve a little for garnishing).

Combine the tahini, lemon juice, garlic and salt and black pepper and stir the mixture into the salad until the beans and tomatoes are well coated. Transfer the salad to a serving dish, garnish it with reserved parsley and serve at once.

INDONESIAN RICE SALAD

This sounds an unlikely choice for a winter salad but all the ingredients are readily available. It brings a hint of the sunny tropics to a gloomy winter's day.

2fl oz (50ml) orange juice
2 tablespoons (30ml) sesame seed or other vegetable oil
2 tablespoons (30ml) soy sauce
Salt and pepper to taste
8oz (225g) long-grain brown or white rice, cooked and cooled to room temperature
2oz (50g) beansprouts, washed
1 medium green pepper, core and seeds removed and chopped
1 stick celery, chopped
2 spring onions, chopped
2oz (50g) roasted almonds or cashews
2oz (50g) sultanas, plumped up with a little boiling water and then drained
4oz (100g) fresh or tinned pineapple chunks

Serves 4-6

Make the dressing. Combine the first 3 ingredients and season to taste. Mix together all the remaining ingredients. Pour the dressing over the salad. Toss well together and chill slightly before serving.

Variations

Serve the salad on a bed of greens.
Add thinly sliced water chestnuts or bamboo shoots.
Garnish the salad with a little dry-roasted desiccated coconut.

Indonesian specialities
Indonesian cuisine includes a variety of unusual dishes, such as Indonesian fruit salad (left) and mixed vegetable salad with peanut sauce, or Gado-gado (right). The beauty of these lovely salads lies in their versatility. Their components can be varied according to the seasonal availability of fruit and vegetables, and they are acceptable both as part of a meal or on their own.

VEGETABLE SALAD WITH PEANUT SAUCE

Gado-gado is one of my favourite Indonesian dishes. It is crunchy, tasty and good for you. It makes a good light lunch or with rice and other side dishes, an excellent vegetarian meal. A mixture of raw and cooked vegetables are arranged on a serving dish and a spicy peanut sauce is either served with them or poured over the top before serving. The reccipe I have given is a general one and you may substitute your own selection of vegetables. The cooked vegetables (except the potatoes) are only parboiled and should retain their texture and colour. Gado-gado can be served hot or cold.

Sauce
2 tablespoons (30ml) vegetable oil
2 cloves garlic, crushed
1-3 (according to taste) fresh or dried red chillies, finely sliced, or ½-1½ teaspoons (2.5-7.5ml) chilli powder
1 medium onion, finely diced
8oz (225g) roasted peanuts, crushed or milled in a food blender or 8oz (225g) crunchy peanut butter
1 tablespoon (15ml) brown sugar
1 tablespoon (15ml) lemon juice
16fl oz (450ml) water
Salt to taste

Vegetables
½ medium cucumber, thickly sliced
4oz (100g) beansprouts, washed, drained
½ lettuce, washed and chopped or 1 small bunch watercress
2 medium carrots, sliced lengthwise, parboiled
2 medium potatoes, peeled and boiled until just cooked, sliced
3oz (75g) cabbage leaves, lightly blanched in boiling water, chopped
4oz (100g) green or french beans, stringed, cut into 2in (5cm) lengths, parboiled

To garnish
choose from:
1 hard-boiled egg, sliced
2 medium onions, thinly sliced and fried crisp and brown in a little oil

Serves 4

To make the sauce, heat the oil in a saucepan or wok and add the garlic, chillies or chilli powder and onion and stir fry the mixture over a moderate heat until the onion is golden.

Add the crushed peanuts or peanut butter, sugar, lemon juice and water, stir well and bring it all to a gentle boil. Reduce the heat and simmer, stirring occasionally, until the sauce has thickened but remains thin enough to pour. Add salt to taste. Keep the sauce hot on a very low simmer.

Prepare and arrange the vegetables on a serving dish, pour the sauce over (or serve it in a separate bowl) and garnish the top with slices of hard-boiled egg and fried onions. The result is an unusual, visually attractive and highly nutritious dish, full of savour.

VEGETABLE DISHES

Vegetables are becoming an increasingly important part of our diet and are no longer confined to playing a minor role in a meal. They should be bought in prime condition and prepared carefully to preserve the natural nutrients they contain.

BROCCOLI WITH MUSTARD SAUCE

3 pints (2 litres) water
1 teaspoon (5ml) salt
llb (450g) broccoli, cut into florettes
2 tablespoons (30ml) dry English mustard
2 tablespoons (30ml) water
2 tablespoons (30ml) soy sauce
2 tablespoons (30ml) sugar
Serves 4

Bring the water to the boil, add salt and parboil the broccoli for three to four minutes. Drain.

Combine the remaining ingredients in a bowl, pour over the broccoli and leave to marinate for one hour.

Serve cold or drain off marinade, heat to boiling, toss in broccoli, heat through and serve at once.

Something special This recipe for creating an unusual broccoli dish with mustard sauce is very simple, but the end result is quite stunning.

ODEN

Oden is a popular winter casserole, often prepared for festive occasions when Japanese people help themselves out of the oden pot, which can bubble away all evening without spoiling. In some big cities, they have vendors in the streets selling oden.

1lb (450g) tofu, deep fried
2 pints (1.1 litres) soup stock
1 teaspoon (5ml) salt
1 tablespoon (15ml) sugar
1 tablespoon (15ml) soy sauce
8oz (225g) daikon (white radish) or small turnip cut into 1in (2.5cm) cubes
1 medium carrot, cut into 2in (5cm) lengths
8 leaves cabbage, coarsely chopped
3 bamboo shoots, cut in half, crosswise
6 small potato es
6 hard-boiled eggs

Prepare the deep-fried tofu as indicated in the recipe for Mixed Vegetables and Tofu; reserve.

Combine the stock, salt, sugar and soy sauce in a large pot and bring to the boil. Add daikon and carrot. Cook for 30 minutes, uncovered. Replenish evaporated liquid with soup stock or water. Add all the other ingredients and simmer slowly for 30 minutes. Invite each person to ladle out some cooking liquid and a selection of vegetables, tofu, etc.

Japanese casserole Oden is ideal to make in the winter, as its ingredients are readily available. The Japanese traditionally eat it on festive occasions and, in some big cities, street vendors do a brisk trade in it all day long.

AUBERGINE SAMOSAS

8oz (225g) wholewheat flour
½ teaspoon (2.5ml) salt
4 tablespoons (60ml) vegetable oil
6-8fl oz (175-225ml) water

Filling
1 large aubergine or 2 small ones, finely chopped, salted for ½ hour, rinsed and drained
Salt
1 tablespoon (15ml) vegetable oil
2 cloves garlic
½ teaspoon (2.5ml) ground allspice
2 tablespoons (30ml) tomato purée
Oil for frying

Serves 4 as a main meal, 8 as an appetiser

First make the dough. Combine the flour and salt in a bowl, stir in 3 tablespoons (45ml) oil and mix well. Add the water a little at a time until you have a firm dough. Knead well for about 10 minutes, until smooth. (If you have a food processor, put the flour, salt and oil into the bowl and with the machine running pour the water in a slow stream through the feed tube, adding just enough to enable the dough to form a ball around the knife. Stop adding liquid and allow the dough to make 10 more turns around the bowl before turning the processor off.) Brush the dough with the remaining oil and cover with a cloth until ready for use.

Make the filling. Sauté the aubergine in the oil with the garlic and allspice until soft. Stir in the tomato purée, season with pepper and cool.

Divide the dough into 16 equal parts and roll each into a ball. Roll out each ball on a well-floured surface to form a 4in (10cm) round.

Spoon a portion of the filling onto each round. Dampen half the circumference of each round and fold the other half over to form half-moon shapes. Press the edges to seal them.

Pour 3 or 4in (7 or 10cm) oil into a deep pan and heat to about 350°F (180°C). Deep fry the samosas a few at a time for 2 to 3 minutes or until golden brown. Remove them from the oil and drain them well on kitchen paper. Serve immediately.

MIXED VEGETABLE AND TOFU

Tofu is an excellent ingredient in mixed vegetable dishes. It absorbs other flavours and links them together.

6oz (175g) tofu, cut into 1in (2.5cm) cubes, oil for deep frying
2 tablespoons (30ml) vegetable oil
1 clove garlic, crushed
1 medium onion, thinly sliced
4oz (100g) cabbage, coarsely chopped
4oz (100g) brocoli, cut into flowerettes and/or 4oz (100g) sprouts, quartered
1 small aubergine, salted, rinsed and drained
2 stalks celery, cut in ½in (1.25cm) lengths
4oz (100g) French beans, cut in 1in (2.5cm) lengths
1 medium green pepper cut in 1in (2.5) strips
1 bamboo shoot, sliced into half moons
1 lotus root, sliced into half moons
2oz (50g) mushrooms, sliced
1 teaspoon (5ml) salt
1 teaspoon (5ml) togarashi or black pepper
2 tablespoons (30ml) soy sauce
10fl oz (275ml) soup stock or water
2 tablespoons (30ml) dry sherry (optional)

Serves 6-8

Heat the oil in a vegetable type casserole, add garlic and sauté for one minute, add onions and lightly brown.

Add all the remaining vegetables and stir fry for three to four minutes. Add remaining ingredients except tofu and sherry and bring to the boil; reduce heat and simmer for ten minutes.

Drop in tofu and simmer for a further ten minutes. Finally add the sherry and serve from casserole.

To deep fry tofu, it must first be pressed to remove excess moisture. Cut the tofu blocks into thick slices. Put the slices between two absorbent towels and place a cutting board or other weight on top. Leave for 30 minutes and then proceed to deep fry.

Pour enough oil into a heavy-bottomed pan or frying pan to come 1in-1½in (2.5-3.75cm) up the sides. Heat pan on a high heat until a small piece of tofu dropped into the fat immediately bubbles (150°-175°C/300°-350°F). Reduce heat slightly and carefully drop in the tofu slices. Deep fry for one or two minutes or until tofu floats to the surface of the oil. Turn slices over and fry another two minutes. Lift from oil and drain on a rack or absorbent towels. You will find that one of the great advantages of tofu is that, while being an extremely healthy food in itself, it will not disguise the flavour and savour of the vegetables you are cooking.

Everyday fare Mixed vegetables with tofu is a tasty, simple dish which makes a nutritious main course. It is perfect for a midday meal, or an informal supper party.

AUBERGINE AND POTATO CURRY

Serve with brown rice and/or chapattis (page 52) and mango chutney.

Spiced vegetables Aubergine and potato curry served with brown rice and chapattis is both delicious and economical. The intensity of the spices can be varied as you wish.

2 tablespoons (30ml) vegetable oil
1 large clove garlic, crushed
½ teaspoon (2.5ml) ginger
½ teaspoon (2.5ml) turmeric
½ teaspoon (2.5ml) cumin seeds
½ teaspoon mustard seed
1 pinch each of cayenne, ground coriander and cinnamon
1 large aubergine, diced in large cubes, salted for ½ hour, rinsed
1 large green pepper, seeded, cored, and cut in large strips
2 large potatoes, scrubbed and cubed
½ pint (275ml) water
4 tomatoes, quartered
½oz (15g) butter or margarine

Serves 4

Heat the oil and sauté the garlic and spices for 5 minutes.

Add the aubergine pieces to the mixture. Cook for 2 minutes, then add the green pepper and potatoes with the water. Bring to the boil, cover, reduce heat and simmer for 30 minutes. Add the tomatoes and butter or margarine. Cook for 2 more minutes and serve at once with rice and/or chappatis.

BROCHETTES WITH RICE AND BRAZIL NUTS

Although vegetable brochettes are baked in this recipe they are equally good grilled under a hot grill or barbecued over charcoal.

Corn on the cob, sliced thickly
2 courgettes, cut into thick rings
12 large mushrooms, washed and left whole
4 large tomatoes, cut in half
1 large green pepper, seeded and cut into 2in (5cm) squares
1 large red pepper, seeded and cut into 2in (5cm) squares
Olive oil
12oz (350g) brown rice
4oz (100g) Brazil nuts, roasted and coarsely chopped
Soya sauce to taste

Serves 4

Preheat oven to 400°F (200°C) gas mark 6.

Divide the corn, courgettes, mushrooms, tomatoes, green and red peppers into four heaps. Place four skewers through the vegetables, kebab style. Brush them with olive oil and lay on a greased baking tray.

Bake for 40 minutes, turning once during the course of baking. In the meantime, cook the rice.

Serve on a bed of hot pilau rice with Brazil nuts sprinkled over. Allow people individually to season their brochettes with soya sauce.

Exotic alternatives Unusual cooking techniques and a little extra effort can transform the humblest vegetables into stunning meals, like these vegetable brochettes with rice and brazil nuts (right), and aubergine samosas (left).

Healthy pastry Vegetable pie with wholemeal walnut pastry served with broccoli spears makes a perfect winter dish. Any vegetables can be used for the filling; you can also ring the changes by varying the ground nuts you use to make the pastry.

VEGETABLE PIE WITH WALNUT PASTRY

A delicious looking pie with a colourful filling. Serve it piping hot with broccoli for a lovely winter meal. The pastry for this pie could also be made with other ground nuts, for instance, hazelnuts, almonds or peanuts (roasted first). You could also substitute other vegetables such as celery, Jeusalem artichokes, leeks or even aubergines, according to personal preference and availability.

4oz (100g) wholemeal flour
1oz (25g) ground walnuts
2oz (50g) margarine or butter
water to mix
2 tablespoons (30ml) vegetable oil
1 large onion, chopped
1 teaspoon (5ml) chopped fresh rosemary or 2.5ml (½ teaspoon dried rosemary)
1 large potato, peeled and chopped
1 large courgette, sliced
8oz (225g) tin sweet corn, drained
8oz (225g) tomatoes, peeled and chopped
Salt and black pepper to taste
1 egg, beaten

Combine the flour and walnuts in a mixing bowl or the container of a food processor. Mix well, rub or blend in the margarine and add enough water (about 4 table spoons (60ml) to form a firm, non-sticky pastry. Wrap the pastry in cling film and set it aside in the refrigerator.

Preheat oven to 400°F (200°C) gas mark 6.

Heat the oil in a large saucepan and sauté the onion and rosemary for 5 minutes. Add the potato, carrot, courgette and sweetcorn and cook for a further 5 minutes over a moderate heat. Add a little water if the contents start to stick to the pan.

Add to tomatoes, salt and black pepper, stir well and simmer for a further 5 minutes.

Transfer the filling to a deep pie approx. 1¾ (1 litre) pie dish. Roll out the pastry 1in (2.5cm) larger than the top of the dish. Cut this strip off and put it in place around the dampened rim of the dish. Dampen the edge of the pastry top and unroll it over the top of the pastry rim. Press the pastry edges together with the tines of a fork.

Brush the top of the pie with beaten egg and bake in the preheated oven for 40 minutes.

STUFFED VEGETABLES

Stuffed vegetables, called mishshi or dolmas, are an intrinsic part of Arab cuisine and nearly every vegetable available to the Middle Eastern cook has been adapted to this way of cooking. There are a host of fillings and as many ways of stuffing and cooking the vegetables. To simplify matters I have decided to give recipes for four different rice-based fillings, plus a description of how to prepare and cook three vegetables suitable for stuffing. Finally there are recipes for tomato sauce and yoghurt sauce, which may be substituted for water as the cooking medium, and for a mishshi garnishing.

STUFFED AUBERGINES

4 medium aubergines, stalks left on
Salt
2 tablespoons (30ml) oil or melted butter
Selected filling
Water or tomato sauce or yoghurt sauce
Garnish, optional

Serves 4

Wash the aubergines complete with stalks and make a deep slit from one end to the other without actually breaking open the end. Press open the slit and and sprinkle liberally with salt. Set the aubergines aside, cut side down for 30 minutes, then rinse and pat dry.

Preheat the oven to 350°F (175°C) gas mark 4.

Heat the oil or butter in a heavy frying pan and fry the aubergines all over until they have softened but have not lost their shape. Grease a casserole dish and put the aubergines into it, open side up. Pack them with the selected filling and pour into the dish enough water or sauce to come half way up the sides of the aubergines.

STUFFED COURGETTES

2lb (900g) medium courgettes, washed
salt
Selected filling
16fl oz (450ml) water or tomato sauce or yoghurt sauce

Garnish, optional

Serves 4

Cut the stem ends off the courgettes and carefully hollow out the centre of each with an apple corer leaving an ⅛-¼in (3-6mm) shell.

Soak the hollowed courgettes in salted water for 10 minutes then drain. Fill them with the filling and then arrange them in a heavy casserole. Add the water or selected sauce and bring the pot to the boil. Cover, reduce the heat and simmer for 30 minutes or until the courgettes are tender. Garnish if wished.

STUFFED PEPPERS

4 medium peppers
2 tablespoons (30ml) oil
selected filling
16fl oz water or tomato sauce
Garnish, optional

Serves 4

Cut the tops off the peppers, remove the seeds and pith. Heat the oil in a heavy frying pan and lightly sauté the peppers all over until they are softened but still retain their shape.

Preheat the oven to 350°F (175°C) gas mark 4.

Stuff the peppers with the selected filling and pack them into a casserole dish. Put the tops back on the pappers and pour into the dish the water or tomato sauce. Bake for 30 minutes or until the peppers and filling are tender. Garnish if wished.

FILLINGS

RICE FILLING

- 2 tablespoons (30ml) oil
- 2 medium onions, finely diced
- 1lb (450g) cooked long-grain rice
- 2 medium tomatoes, peeled and chopped
- 2 tablespoons (30ml) freshly chopped parsley or mint or coriander
- ½ teaspoon (2.5ml) allspice
- ½ teaspoon (2.5ml) cinnamon
- Salt and black pepper to taste
- 2oz (50g) raisins or sultanas presoaked and drained (optional)

Lightly fry the onion in the oil, then combine it with all the other ingredients and mix well. The onion and spices add savour, while the raisins are an attractive extra.

Vegetable cornucopia
Stuffed vegetables of every variety, such as peppers (top left), courgettes (right), and aubergines (bottom left), play an important part in Middle Eastern cookery. Its keynotes are style, versatility and cooking simplicity.The combination of vegetable, filling and garnish can be altered according to personal taste and the availability of the raw ingredients.

Variations

RICE AND CHICKPEA FILLING

Replace half the rice in the above recipe with 8oz (225g) cooked, drained chick-peas.

RICE AND NUT FILLING

Substitute the tomatoes in the above recipes with 4oz (100g) pine nuts, blanched almonds, chopped walnuts or pistachios.

RICE AND DRIED FRUIT FILLING

Any combination of dried fruits, such as prunes, apricots, pears or apples, may be used in this variation. As well as the fruits and some cooked long-grain rice, you will need a diced medium onion, sultanas – these should be presoaked and drained – and the juice of a lemon. Season the filling with mint – freshly chopped mint is best, though dried mint can substitute – a little cinnamon and allspice and salt and black pepper to taste.

Lightly fry the onion in oil. Then combine it with the other ingredients, mixing them well together until cooked.

SAUCES

TOMATO SAUCE

2 tablespoons (30ml) oil or melted butter
2 medium onions, finely chopped
4 cloves garlic, crushed
8oz (225g) fresh or tinned tomatoes, chopped
2oz (50g) tomato purée
8fl oz (225ml) water
1 teaspoon (5ml) crushed oregano
½ teaspoon (2.5ml) cinnamon
Salt and black pepper to taste

Heat the oil or butter in a heavy frying pan and sauté the onion and garlic until softened. Add the remaining ingredients, mix well, bring to the boil and gently simmer for 5 minutes. Garnish if wished.

YOGHURT SAUCE

Cows'-milk yoghurt curdles if it is cooked for any length of time or if it is boiled. Thus unless it is going to be added to a dish just before it is to be served, it must be stabilized for use as a cooking sauce. This is not the case with goats'-milk yoghurt, which curdles much less readily.

16fl oz (450ml) plain yoghurt
1 egg white
½ teaspoon (2.5ml) salt

Put the yoghurt into a small heavy pan, beat the egg white until it is just frothy and stir it over a low heat into the yoghurt along with the salt. Continue stirring, always in the same direction, until the mixture just boils. Reduce the heat to very low and leave it to simmer uncovered for 5 minutes or until it has become th[ck. The yoghurt may now be cooked without it curdling.

GARNISHES FOR STUFFED VEGETABLES

½ teaspoon (2.5ml) salt
2 cloves garlic, crushed
1 teaspoon (5ml) dried
crushed mint
juice of 1 lemon

In a pestle and mortar crush together the salt, garlic and mint. Stir in the lemon juice and sprinkle the mixture over hot stuffed vegetables before serving.

Variations

If there is no time to make the above garnishing just sprinkle the cooked dish of stuffed vegetables with fresh lemon juice and/or chopped fresh herbs or crushed dried herbs.

Cabbage with a difference
Hot slaw is an unusual variation on standard winter cabbage dishes. The hot sour cream sauce can be used to heat the cabbage through, or simply poured over the raw shredded vegetable.

HOT SLAW

Cabbage salad or cole-slaw is well known, but an unusual vegetable dish is fresh shredded cabbage served in a hot sour cream sauce. The cabbage can be heated through in the sauce and served very hot, or just covered in the sauce and served right away. In the first method the cabbage loses some of its crispness but the dish is very nice for a cold winter's day. In the second method the cabbage retains its texture and served in this way it is an excellent spring or summer vegetable dish.

4 tablespoons (60ml) wine vinegar
1 tablespoon (15ml) sunflower or other vegetable oil
1 tablespoon (15ml) honey
1 teaspoon (5ml) prepared English mustard
2 medium egg yolks
2 tablespoonS (30ml) milk
Salt to taste
2fl oz (50ml) sour cream
1lb (450g) crisp white cabbage, finely shredded
or
12oz (350g) crisp white cabbage, finely shredded and 4oz (100g) crisp red cabbage, finely shredded
1 medium eating apple, cored, finely chopped
Freshly milled black pepper

Serves 4

Put the first six ingredients in a blender or food processor and process to a smooth liquid. Put the liquid into the top of a double boiler over boiling water, or in a heavy small pan over a very low heat. Stirring all the time, cook the liquid until it thickens to the consistency of a thin sauce. Salt to taste. Put the sour cream in a bowl and stir into it 2 tablespoons (30ml) of the prepared sauce. Slowly pour the whole of this mixture back into the main sauce in the pan and heat with stirring until very hot.

Combine the shredded cabbage and apple and pour the sauce over. Mill some black pepper over the top and serve.

Alternatively, heat the cabbage through in the sauce in a pan or frying pan and then serve seasoned with black pepper.

Turkish delight Turkish vegetable casserole is a delicious multi-flavoured dish. Serve with yoghurt for a traditional Turkish meal.

TURKISH VEGETABLE CASSEROLE

2oz (50g) butter
2 medium aubergines, thickly sliced, salted, rinsed and drained
2 medium green peppers, seeded cored and thickly sliced
2 medium courgettes, thickly sliced
8oz (225g) tomatoes, sliced
8oz (225g) French beans oz other green beans, cut in 2in (5cm) pieces
4 cloves garlic finely chopped
10fl oz (275ml) water or stock
Salt and black pepper to taste
8fl oz (225ml) yoghurt

Preheat the oven to 350°F (175°C) gas mark 4.

Melt the butter in a heavy frying pan and lightly brown the aubergines on both sides. Transfer to a baking dish. Add the other vegetables to the frying pan and lightly sauté them, stirring. Add the vegetables to the aubergines and add the garlic, water or stock and salt and black pepper to taste. Cover and bake in the oven for 1 hour or longer. Serve with a separate bowl of yoghurt.

RICE AND GRAINS

Rice and cereal grains are major sources of protein for vegetarians; this chapter includes a variety of recipes from countries as far apart as Japan, Morocco, Spain, Egypt and Iran. Make sure, whenever you can, that you buy whole or brown rice, wholewheat pasta and so on – they contain more nutrients than the processed types.

LASAGNE COVENT GARDEN

For a nutritious, and delicious, meal, serve this dish with wholemeal bread and a salad.

12oz (350g) carrots, peeled and sliced
12oz (350ml) parsnips, peeled and sliced
½oz (15g) butter or margarine
Salt and freshly ground black pepper to taste
6 sheets fresh or pre-cooked wholemeal lasagne
12oz (350g) cottage cheese
2oz (50g) walnuts, roughly chopped
2lb (900g) fresh spinach, cooked soft in a little water of 1lb (450g) frozen spinach, thawed, drained well, chopped
¼ teaspoon (1.25ml) nutmeg
4oz (100g) mozzarella cheese, sliced thinly
1 large tomato, sliced thinly
fresh or dried basil

Serves 8

Preheat the oven to 350°F (180°C) gas mark 4. Cook the carrots in a large saucepan, containing enough boiling salted water to cover, for 5 minutes, then add the parsnips and continue cooking for a further 10 minutes or until both vegetables are very tender.

Drain the vegetables well and mash together with the butter; season with salt and pepper. Spread the mixture onto the base of an ovenproof dish.

Cover it with three sheets of the lasagne (uncooked), then with the cottage cheese mixed with the chopped walnuts. Cover this layer with the remaining lasagne. Spread over this the spinach seasoned with nutmeg, salt and pepper. Place the cheese slices over the top and bake

London pasta Lasagne dishes are always popular and very sustaining. Serve this delicious version – Lasagne Covent Garden – with pear and watercress salad.

in the oven for 30 minutes or until the lasagne is tender and the cheese golden brown.

Remove from the oven and decorate with slices of tomato and fresh basil.

IRANIAN VEGETABLE POLO

This exotic blend of fruit and vegetables is the Iranian, and some say original, version of pilau rice. It is traditionally cooked on the top of the stove, but can equally well be baked in the oven. Instructions for both methods are given.

1lb (450g) long-grain rice, soaked in water for 4-6 hours or overnight
1 tablespoon (15ml) salt
3½ pints (2 litres) water
4 tablespoons (60ml) butter or vegetable oil
2 medium onions, thinly sliced
1 medium green pepper, seeded, cored and sliced
1 clove garlic, crushed
2 medium carrots, thinly sliced
4oz (100g) garden peas, fresh or frozen
2oz (50g) dried apricots, soaked overnight, drained and chopped
2oz (50g) raisins, soaked 1 hour and drained
2oz (50g) blanched almonds or other nuts
2 tablespoons (30ml) grated orange peel
1 teaspoon (5ml) ground cinnamon
½ teaspoon (2.5ml) ground nutmeg
Salt and black pepper to taste
4fl oz (100ml) water or stock

Serves 6-8

Drain the rice well and wash it under running cold water until the water runs clear. Drain again. Add the salt and boil rapidly for 8 minutes or until the rice is not quite tender. At this stage the centre of a rice grain should not be hard, but the rice should still be a little chewy. Drain the rice, rinse with a little warm water and drain again. Melt half the butter in a heavy frying pan and add the onions, pepper, garlic and carrots. Cook them, stirring occasionally, for five minutes or until the vegetables are just softened. Add the peas and continue cooking another three to four minutes. Season to taste.

In another pan, melt half the remaining butter and cook in it the apricots, raisins, almonds, orange peel, cinnamon and nutmeg for 5 minutes, stirring occasionally. Coat the bottom of a big, heavy pan (the pan can be replaced by a casserole dish and the polo is then baked in a preheated oven at 350°F (175°C) gas mark 4 for 30 minutes) with the remaining butter and spread half of the parboiled rice over this. Cover with the onions and vegetable mixture. Spread half the remaining rice over this, and on top spread the fruit and nut mixture. Top with the remaining rice, pour in the water or stock and cover the pan with a tight-fitting lid or use a lid wrapped in a clean tea towel with the ends tucked in. Simmer over a low heat for 20 to 25 minutes, and then tip the polo on to a large serving dish.

NORIMAKI-SUSHI

Norimaki-sushi is rice and other ingredients wrapped in a thin sheet of nori seaweed. The resulting Swiss roll shape is cut into thick slices. The fillings are prepared before the sushi is rolled in the seaweed wrapping. For clarity this recipe is divided into three parts. First make the sushi rice. Then prepare the chosen fillings and lastly assemble the norimaki. The amounts given for each filling will norimaki for four to six people.

SUSHI RICE

The quantities given in this recipe may not be suitable for all types of rice, and you may need to experiment a little to find the exact combination of cooking water and sugar/vinegar mixture to give the best sushi rice. Do remember the success of the dish depends on the quality of the sushi rice. It should be tasty, sticky enough to mould, but not the least bit squashy or mashed up.

The quantities given for the sushi dressing will make enough for several preparations of sushi rice. Reserve what you do not use and store in the refrigerator. It also makes an ideal base for rice salads.

4fl oz (100ml) vinegar
6oz (175g) sugar
1 tablespoon (15ml) salt
1lb (450g) rice, washed and drained
1½ pints (850ml) water

To prepare sushi dressing, combine vinegar, sugar and salt and bring to the boil. Turn off heat and leave. Use hot or cold; either way it gives the same result.

Place the rice in a heavy pan. Add the water, cover the pan and bring to the boil quickly. Turn the heat right down and allow it to simmer for 15 minutes. Remove from the heat and allow to stand for 5-10 minutes. Turn it into a wooden or non-metallic bowl.

Pour 2-3 tablespoons (30-45ml) dressing over the hot rice until a little remains unabsorbed in the bottom of the bowl. Now stir the rice gently with a wet rice paddle or wooden spoon. Set aside while you prepare the fillings.

NORIMAKI-SUSHI FILLINGS

Here are a few ideas for fillings for norimaki-sushi which can, of course, be supplemented with your own ideas. Make full use of leftover cooked vegetables.

Creativity with rice Norimaki sushi. This Japanese dish makes a really unusual meal – delicious, and attractive to the eye. The various different fillings allow for innovation in colour and flavour.

CARROT FILLING

1 medium carrot, quartered lengthwise and cut into ¼in (0.5cm) thick sticks
1 tablespoon (15ml) vegetable oil
1 tablespoon (15ml) water
Pinch of salt

Sauté the carrot sticks in the oil for two minutes. Add water and pinch of salt. Simmer unitl carrots are just soft.

SPINACH FILLING

4oz (100g) spinach
2 tablespoons (30ml) water
Pinch of salt
1 tablespoon (15ml) sesame seeds, toasted

Boil spinach lightly in salted water for two to three minutes. Drain well, chop and mix with sesame seeds

EGG FILLING

Beat 2 eggs. Prepare paper-thin omelettes and cut into ¼in (0.5cm) wide strips

MUSHROOM FILLING

4oz (100g) mushrooms, thinly sliced
4 tablespoons (60ml) water
1½ teaspoons (7.5ml) sugar
1½ teaspoons (7.5ml) soy sauce

Cook the mushrooms in the remaining ingredients for 5 minutes or until soft.

Nutritious noodles Noodles are a pleasant alternative to rice or pasta, and come in several different textures. These Oriental-style dishes, fried buckwheat noodles with spinach (left), and soft fried udon noodles (right), are wholesome and very appetising.

FRIED BUCKWHEAT NOODLES WITH SPINACH

2 tablespoons (30ml) oil
4 cloves garlic, crushed
1lb (450g) fresh spinach, washed, coarsely chopped and drained
12oz (350g) buckwheat noodles, cooked
Salt and black pepper to taste

Heat the oil in a heavy pan. Add the garlic and sauté until light brown (about 3 minutes). Add the spinach, cover the pan and lower the heat. Simmer until the spinach is completely wilted, stirring occasionally.

Now stir in noodles, season with salt and black pepper and heat through. Serve.

VEGETABLE COUSCOUS

Couscous is a wheat grain product made from semolina, and it is also the name of the famous dish of which couscous is the main ingredient. The couscous is steamed over a rich sauce or stew and then served in a mountainous heap with the sauce poured over it.

2oz (50g) butter or vegetable oil
3 cloves garlic, crushed
2 medium onions, quartered
6 small courgettes, cut in 1in (2.5cm) pieces
2 medium green peppers, seeded, cored and cut into thick strips
2 large potatoes, scrubbed or peeled, and coarsely chopped
4 medium carrots, peeled, cut in half crosswise, then sliced lengthwise
2 small turnips, cut in half then sliced lengthwise
3 pints (1.6 litres) water
1lb (450g) couscous
8oz (225g) chickpeas, cooked and drained
1lb (450g) fresh tomatoes, quartered or 1lb (450g) tinned tomatoes
4oz (100g) sultanas, apricots or raisins, soaked and drained
1½ teaspoons (7.5ml) ground coriander
1½ teaspoons (7.5ml) ground cumin
2 teaspoons (10ml) turmeric
1½ teaspoons (7.5ml) cayenne
1-2 small chilli peppers, seeded, chopped
Salt and black pepper to taste
Hot pepper sauce or harissa
Garnish
2 eggs, hard boiled, shelled, sliced

Serves 6-8

In a heavy saucepan or in the bottom of a couscousier melt the butter, add the next seven ingredients and sauté, stirring, over a moderate heat for 5 minutes. Add 1 pint (575ml) water and bring to the boil. Reduce the heat and set to simmer.

Meanwhile, place the couscous in a large bowl and gently stir in 1 pint (575ml) cold water. Drain immediately and allow the wet grains to stand for 10 minutes. As they swell up, rake them with your fingers.

Turn the grains into the top of a couscousier or into a colander and place it over the cooking vegetables. Leave to steam gently for 20 minutes. Remove the top of the couscousier or the colander and add to the cooking vegetables the remaining ingredients (except the garnish) and 1 pint (575 ml) water. Return the vegetables to the boil and then reduce the heat and simmer for 15 minutes. Stir the couscous grains to break up any lumps that have formed and put the couscous back over the cooking vegetables. Cook and steam for a final 15 minutes.

Pile the grains on a large serving dish. Drain off some of the liquid from the vegetables into a separate bowl. Pour the vegetables over the couscous and serve with the cooking liquid and a hot pepper sauce or harissa in separate bowls. Finally, garnish with slices of egg.

Arabian nights Vegetable couscous. The exotic colours of this dish add to its appeal, and make it ideal to serve at a party. A delicious way to sample traditional Arab cuisine.

RICE, NOODLES AND LENTILS WITH SAUCE

This Egyptian recipe makes a substantial meal. Serve with fresh, crisp, green salad and a bowl of plain yoghurt.

4 tablespoons (60ml) oil
1 medium onion, finely diced
1 clove garlic, crushed
½ teaspoon (2.5ml) turmeric
8oz (225g) long-grain rice, washed and drained
8oz (225g) thin noodles, broken into pieces
2oz (50g) sultanas or raisins, plumped up in hot water, drained (optional)
16fl oz (450ml) boiling water
Salt and black pepper to taste
8oz (225g) cooked, drained brown lentils

Tomato Sauce
1 medium onion, finely diced
2 cloves garlic, crushed
2 tablespoons (30ml) oil
3 tablespoons (45ml) tomato purée
10fl oz (275ml) water
Salt and black pepper to taste

Heat the oil in a large heavy frying pan and sauté the onion and garlic until just softened. Stir in the turmeric and then the rice and noodles. Stir and gently cook until the rice and pasta are coated in oil and lightly browned. Add the raisins if used, pour in the boiling water and season to taste with salt and black pepper. Reduce the heat to low and simmer until the rice is tender and all the liquid absorbed.

Meanwhile, make the tomato sauce. Sauté the onion and garlic in the oil until softened and lightly browned. Stir in the tomato purée, water and seasoning. Mix well, bring to the boil, reduce the heat and simmer for a few minutes. Keep hot.

Fold the cooked lentils into the rice mixture and transfer to a heated serving dish. Serve with tomato sauce.

SOFT FRIED UDON OR SOBA NOODLES

Japanese udon are fat noodles made from wheatflour, while soba are buckwheat flour noodles. They tend to be a little chewier and tastier than the wheatflour variety, and are, perhaps, Japan's favourite noodle.

This is a basic recipe; more elaborate additions are suggested below.

4 tablespoons (60ml) vegetable oil
1 clove garlic, minced
25g (1oz) fresh ginger root, grated (optional)
½ medium carrot, grated
100g (4oz) Chinese cabbage, chopped
1 medium green pepper, diced
12oz (350g) udon or soba, cooked (see packet for details) and drained
Black pepper to taste
Soy sauce to taste

Heat the oil in a heavy frying pan, sauté the garlic and ginger for 2 to 3 minutes, then add the other vegetables. Fry until just soft cooked. Stir in the noodles, heat through, season with soy sauce and pepper.

Other ingredients that can be fried with noodles are:

- 2 paper-thin omelettes cut into 1in (2.5cm) strips
- 4oz (100g) French beans, cut into 1in (2.5cm) pieces
- 2 stalks celery, chopped
- 1 medium onion, diced
- 2 spring onions, chopped
- 4oz (100g) bean sprouts
- 1 medium lotus, sliced, or bamboo shoots
- 2oz (50g) mushrooms, sliced
- 4 shiitake (Japanese dried mushrooms) soaked for 20 minutes, hard stems removed, sliced
- 6oz (175g) tofu, 1in (2.5cm) cubes
- 6oz (175g) fried tofu, cut into 1/2in (1.25cm) cubes

4oz (100g) cheese, grated

RICE STEW WITH YOGURT AND VEGETABLES

4 tablespoons (60ml) vegetable oil
3 medium onions, thinly sliced
3 tablespoons (45ml) split red lentils
8oz (225g) rice
2 pints (5 cups) water
1lb (450g) fresh spinach, chopped
1 teaspoon (5ml) ground coriander
1 tablespoon (15ml) fresh parsley, chopped
Salt and black pepper to taste
1 medium onion, diced
1 teaspoon (5ml) dried mint
8fl oz (225ml) natural yogurt

Serves 4

Heat 3 tablespoons (45ml) oil in a heavy pan, add the sliced onions and sauté until lightly browned. Stir in the lentils and the rice, add the water and bring to the boil. Reduce the heat, cover and simmer for 20 minutes.

Now add the spinach, coriander, parsley and salt and pepper to taste, and continue cooking a further 30 minutes.

Meanwhile, fry the diced onion in the remaining oil until well browned, sprinkle on the mint and fry for a further minute.

Pour the stew into a serving bowl, beat in the yoghurt, garnish with the mint and fried onion and serve at once.

VEGETABLE KICHIRI

The English breakfast dish kedgeree was derived from this Indian recipe in which lentils, rice and vegetables are cooked together in one pot. Serve with wholemeal chappatis, if you wish.

2 tablespoons (30ml) vegetable oil
1 medium onion, thinly sliced
1 medium carrot, grated
8oz (225g) long-grain brown rice, washed and drained
4oz (100g) green or brown lentils, soaked overnight, drained
2 tablespoons (30ml) dessicated coconut, lightly dry roasted
1 teaspoon (5ml) cumin seeds
1 teaspoon (5ml) powdered cinnamon
½ teaspoon (2.5ml) ground turmeric
¼ teaspoon (1.25ml) ground cloves
1½ pints (850ml) water, boiling
Salt to taste

Garnish
1 banana, sliced
2oz (50g) roasted almonds or peanuts

Heat the oil in a large pan and sauté the onion until just soft; add the carrots and continue sautéing until the onions are coloured light brown. Put in the rice and lentils and fry over a low heat, stirring, for 5 minutes. Add the coconut and spices, mix well and cook, stirring for a further 2 minutes.

Pour in the water, mix, season to taste with salt. Reduce the heat to as low as possible, cover the pan and simmer for 45 to 50 minutes or until all the liquid is absorbed and the rice and lentils are tender. Garnish and serve.

CHINESE-STYLE WHOLEWHEAT

Once the wheat is cooked this wholewheat version of Chinese fried rice is a very quick dish to prepare.

2 pints (1.1 litres) water
1lb (450g) wholewheat berries, soaked for 3-4 hours and drained
1 teaspoon (5ml) salt
2 eggs
1 tablespoon (15ml) butter
4 tablespoons (60ml) vegetable oil
1 medium onion, finely chopped
3 sticks celery, diced
2 green or red peppers, cored, seeded, diced
4oz (100g) mushrooms, diced
4 teaspoons (60ml) soy sauce
Salt and black pepper to taste

Serves 4

Bring the water to a rolling boil. Add the wheat and return to the boil; reduce the heat and simmer for 1½ hours or until the wheat is cooked to the softness you require. Add salt towards the end of cooking time. To speed up the cooking time, dry roast the wheat in a hot frying pan for two to three minutes before adding it to the boiling water. Drain and set aside. Beat the eggs together, heat the butter in a large frying pan, and prepare two thin omelettes. Cut the omelettes into thin strips and set aside.

Heat the oil in the frying pan. When it is hot, add the onion, celery and peppers and sauté until nearly tender. Now add the cooked wholewheat and mushrooms and cook, stirring constantly, for a further five minutes. Just before serving mix in the egg strips, soy sauce, salt and black pepper. Serve immediately.

Perfect paella The distinctive flavours of the nuts and vegetables permeate the rice in this vegetarian version of the famous Spanish classic. Delicious alone, or served with a crisp green salad.

VEGETABLE PAELLA

Paella is a famous Spanish dish named after the large flat two handled pan in which it is cooked. The pan doubles as a serving dish. A large frying pan and a serving dish do the job just as well, although a little of the drama of bringing the food straight from the stove to the table is lost. Normally, paella is cooked with meat and fish; here nuts and cheese provide the protein content.

3 tablespoons (45ml) vegetable oil
2 cloves garlic, crushed
2 medium onions, sliced
2 medium green peppers, cored, seeded, sliced
2 medium tomatoes, chopped
12oz (375g) long grain brown rice
1½ pints (850ml) water or vegetable stock
Salt and black pepper to taste
4oz (100g) cucumber, peeled and sliced
2 sticks celery, chopped
4oz (100g) chopped nuts
2oz (50g) olives
6oz (175g) Cheddar cheese, grated

Serves 4

Heat the oil in a heavy frying pan and sauté the garlic and onions until they start to colour. Add the pepper and sauté for a further 2 to 3 minutes. Stir in the tomatoes and rice and cook over a low heat, stirring, for 5 minutes.

Pour in the water or stock, season with salt and black pepper and boil rapidly for 5 minutes. Add the cucumber, celery and chopped nuts, reduce the heat to a simmer and cook until the rice is tender and all the liquid is absorbed. Serve garnished with olives and cheese.

BURGHUL WHEAT AND AUBERGINE PILAU

Salt
2 medium aubergines, cubed
7oz (225g) butter
1 medium onion, finely chopped
1lb (450g) burghul wheat
Water or stock
Salt and black pepper to taste
2oz (50g) pine nuts
3 tablespoons (45ml) chopped parsley
Plain yoghurt

Serves 4

Salt the aubergines and set them aside in a colander for 30 minutes.

Meanwhile, prepare the pilau. Melt 4oz (100g) butter in a heavy pan and sautè the finely chopped onion until it is well softened.

Measure the burghul by volume and then stir it into the pan. Cook and stir for 2-3 minutes and pour in twice the volume of water or stock. Add salt and black pepper to taste, bring to the boil, reduce the heat to very low, simmer and cook gently for 20-25 minutes or until all the liquid is absorbed and the wheat is tender. Sauté the pine nuts in the remaining butter and set aside.

Rinse the aubergines in cold water and pat dry on absorbent paper. Cook them in 2oz (50g) butter, turning, until they are tender, and then stir in the pine nuts and parsley. Fold this mixture into the burghul and serve with a bowl of plain yoghurt.

FESTIVE RICE CONE (NASI TUMPENG)

One of the dishes always seen at an Indonesian celebration or festivity is a conical shaped mound of yellow rice beautifully decorated with a variety of foods including flower-shaped chillies.

As well as the basic recipe for the rice cone, I have made some suggestions for suitable garnishes. The quantities given will make rice for up to eight people and so the recipe is excellent as a party dish. As you can see, it makes a dramatic table centrepiece.

2 tablespoons (30ml) vegetable oil
1 large onion finely diced
2 cloves garlic, crushed
2lb (1kg) long-grain white rice, washed and drained
1½ pints (850ml) water
1½ pints (850ml) fresh or canned coconut milk
1 teaspoon (5ml) grated lemon rind or chopped lemon grass
4 bay leaves
2 teaspoons (10ml) ground turmeric
3 teaspoons (15ml) salt

Indonesian delight. This festive rice cone is traditionally made at times of celebration in Indonesia. The brilliant colours of the rice and the decorative vegetables make it perfect for parties.

Garnish
select from:
Fresh red chillies, cut into flower shapes (see method below)
Fresh green chillies, seeded, cut into strips
Strips of omelette
Roasted peanuts
Cucumber slices
Salad vegetables, chopped or shredded

Serves 8

Heat the oil in a heavy saucepan and sauté the onion and garlic until golden. Add the rice and stir it over the heat for a couple of minutes.

Slowly pour in the water and then the coconut milk. Mix well and add the lemon rind or lemon grass, bay leaves, turmeric and salt. Bring the rice to the boil slowly, stirring constantly. Cover the pan with a tightly-fitting lid and gently simmer for 20 minutes.

Remove the pan from the heat, stir the contents and then set the pan aside, off the heat, for 5 minutes. The rice is now ready. Arrange it in a cone shape (a conical shaped sieve is good for helping to do this) on a serving dish and garnish.

Note: To make chilli flowers, slit the chillies two or three times vertically from tip almost to base. Drop them into iced water and the strips will curl.

PULSES

Beans, peas and lentils, as a group, are known as pulses or legumes. These are the seeds of plants belonging to the Leguminosae family and, together with cereal grains, are the earliest and still one of the most important of man's food crops. They are an excellent source of proteins, crabohydrates, vitamins and minerals, while, together with grains, they provide all our essential amino acids.

Beans, peas and lentils are nearly always sold in their dried form and they need to be well soaked, preferably overnight, before cooking. They are then drained, covered in fresh water, brought to the boil, covered and simmered until tender. The recipes given here cover a wide range of the types of dishes that can be prepared from them – from casseroles, stews and beanpots to pilau, lasagne and enchiladas. Some recipes given earlier in the Starters and Dips section also contain a number of bean dips.

FASOULIA

8oz (225g) haricot beans, soaked overnight and drained
4fl oz (100ml) olive oil
1 small bulb of garlic cloves, peeled and crushed
1 bay leaf
1 teaspoon (5ml) oregano
2 tablespoons (30ml) tomato purée
Salt and black pepper to taste
Juice of 1 lemon
½ small onion, diced

Serves 4

Put the beans, oil, garlic, bay leaf and oregano into a heavy pot and simmer over a low heat for 15 minutes. Remove from the heat and carefully pour in enough

Beanfeasting Serve nourishing fasoulia with warm, crusty bread for a good, filling meal.

boiling water to cover the beans by about 1in (2.5cm). Stir in the tomato purée and simmer the mixture, covered, over a very low heat for 2 to 2½ hours.

Finally, season to taste with salt and black pepper, sprinkle in the lemon juice and serve garnished with diced raw onion.

FRIED VEGETABLES AND MUNG BEANS

Oriental beans For a light, delicately-flavoured treat, serve Chinese fried vegetables and mung beans with brown rice. Simple and quick to prepare, it can turn an impromptu snack into something special.

8oz (225g) mung beans
1 pint (0.5 litres) water 2 tablespoons (30ml) vegetable oil 1 clove garlic, crushed 1 medium onion, sliced
1 medium green pepper, diced
2 medium courgettes, sliced
4oz (100g) mushrooms, sliced
2 teaspoons (10ml) ground ginger
1 tablespoon (15ml) honey
2 tablespoons (30ml) soy sauce
1 tablesoon (15ml) cornflour

Soak the mung beans in the water for 2 to 4 hours and then simmer in the same water for 40 to 45 minutes or until tender. Drain and set the beans aside.

Heat the vegetable oil in a heavy frying pan or wok and stir fry the garlic, onion, green pepper and courgettes until softened. Add the mushrooms and stir fry a further minute. Blend together the ginger, honey, soy sauce and cornflour and pour the mixture over the vegetables. Add the mung beans and mix well. Stir and cook a further 3 to 4 minutes and serve over hot boiled brown rice.

CHICKPEAS SPANISH STYLE

1lb (450g) chickpeas, soaked overnight, drained
2 pints (1.1 litres) water
3 tablespoons (45ml) vegetable oil (olive oil if possible)
1 medium onion, diced
3 cloves garlic, crushed
1 medium green pepper, chopped
1lb (450g) fresh or tinned tomatoes, chopped
½-1 dried or fresh chilli, finely chopped or ½-1 teaspoon (2.5ml-5ml) hot pepper sauce
1 tablespoon (15ml) fresh parsley, chopped
Salt to taste

Serves 4

Put the chickpeas, water and 1 tablespoon (15ml) oil in a large saucepan and bring to the boil, cover, reduce heat and simmer.

Meanwhile, sauté the onion and garlic until golden in the remaining oil in a frying pan. Add the green pepper and cook until soft. Add the remaining ingredients to the frying pan, stir well, and gently simmer the mixture for 20 to 30 minutes. As the chickpeas approach tenderness (after about 1 hour) add this tomato sauce to them and continue cooking until the chickpeas are tender. Serve.

Winter warm-up This rich, aromatic red bean and burgundy casserole is just the thing to serve on a cold winter's night.

RED BEAN AND BURGUNDY CASSEROLE

A rich and filling casserole with a tempting aroma. This is a good dish to serve on a cold winter's night.

2 tablespoons (30ml) vegetable oil
2 medium onions, coarsely chopped
2 cloves garlic, crushed
2 teaspoons (10ml) cumin seeds
1 teaspoon (5ml) dried oregano
18oz (500g) cooked red kidney beans (about 6oz/175g when dry)
6oz (175g) brown or green lentils, soaked in cold water for 1 hour, drained
4 medium potatoes, peeled and cut into large chunks
10fl oz (350ml) red wine
16fl oz (450ml) water
1 bay leaf
1 teaspoon (5ml) dried thyme
14oz (400g) tinned tomatoes
8oz (225g) carrots, peeled, sliced
1 small cauliflower, broken into florets
5oz (150g) button mushrooms, sliced
8oz (225g) leeks, sliced
Salt and pepper
Finely chopped parsley

Heat the oil in a large saucepan, add the onion and cook until soft. Add the garlic, cumin and oregano and cook for a further 2 minutes. Add the kidney beans, lentils, potatoes, wine, water, bay leaf and thyme. Simmer for 10 minutes. Add the tomatoes and carrots. Cook for another ten minutes and add the cauliflower. Again, after ten minutes add the mushrooms and leeks and simmer for a further 10 minutes.

Season with salt and pepper and sprinkle the parsley over.

ITALIAN BEANS

1lb (450g) haricot beans, soaked overnight, drained
1 clove garlic, crushed
1 small onion, thinly sliced
1 medium green pepper, cored, seeded, thinly sliced
2 tablespoons (30ml) tomato purée
16fl oz (450ml) water
2 tablespoons (30ml) olive oil
2 tablespoons (30ml) fresh parsley, chopped
8 green olives, stoned, chopped
4oz (100g) Parmesan or Cheddar cheese, grated
Salt to taste

Serves 4

Preheat the oven to 325°F (170°F) gas mark 3. Combine beans with all the ingredients except the cheese and salt and place them in a heavy casserole dish. Cover and bring to the boil. Transfer to the oven and bake for 2 hours. Salt to taste and sprinkle cheese over the top. Bake, uncovered, for a further 30 minutes or until the cheese melts and browns.

CHILLI BEANS

1 tablespoon (15ml) vegetable oil
1 small onion, chopped
2 cloves garlic, crushed
1 dried chilli, seeded and finely chopped or 1-2 teaspoons (5-10ml) chilli sauce
14oz (400g) canned tomatoes, drained and chopped
½ teaspoon (2.5ml) honey
½ teaspoon (2.5ml) ground cumin
½ teaspoon (2.5ml) dried oregano
½ teaspoon (2.5ml) dried basil
½ teaspoon (2.5ml) ground coriander
Salt and black pepper
1½lb (700g) cooked kidney beans, drained (8oz/225g weight) uncooked
2 tablespoons (30ml) bulgar or burghul wheat
4fl oz (100ml) water

Serves 6

Heat the oil in a saucepan, add the onions, garlic, and chilli. Cook until soft, then add the tomatoes, honey, cumin, oregano, basil, coriander and season with salt and pepper. Cook gently for 5 minutes.

Add the beans, bulgar wheat and water. Bring to the boil, cover and simmer for 30 to 45 minutes or until thick, stirring occasionally.

FRIED BEAN CURD

Oil for deep frying
4 cakes fresh, medium hard bean curd about 4oz (100g) each, cut into 1in (2.5cm) cubes
2 tablespoons (30 ml) dark soya sauce
2fl oz (50ml) soya sauce
3 tablespoons (45ml) crunchy peanut butter
2 cloves garlic
1-2 fresh or dried red chillies
2 tablespoons lemon juice
2 tablespoons (30ml) water
1 teaspoon (5ml) salt
4oz (100g) beansprouts
4oz (100g) cabbage, shredded
½ cucumber, peeled, seeded and diced

To garnish:

4 spring onions, chopped

Serves 4

Heat the oil about 2in (5cm) deep – in a frying pan and deep fry the bean curd cubes, a portion at a time, until crisp and golden brown on all sides. Remove them from the pan with a slotted spoon and drain on absorbent kitchen paper. Keep the bean curd warm in a hot oven. Put the soya sauce, peanut butter, garlic, chillies, lemon juice, water and salt into a blender or food processor and blend the mixture to a smooth consistency. Remove all but about 2 tablespoons of oil from the frying pan in which the bean curd was fried.

Add the sauce and stir fry over a moderate heat for 4-5 minutes. Remove from the heat. Lightly blanch the beansprouts and cabbage separately in fast boiling water and drain them. Put the fried bean curd onto a serving dish, surround it with beansprouts and cabbage, sprinkle over the diced cucumber, cover with sauce and garnish with spring onions. Serve.

BEAN AND CIDER CASSEROLE

2 tablespoons (30ml) vegetable oil
2 cloves garlic, crushed
2 medium onions, sliced
1 medium green pepper, diced
2 medium courgettes (zucchini), sliced
1 bayleaf
2 tablespoons (30ml) tomato purée
½lb (225g) cooked kidney beans
Salt and black pepper to taste
8fl oz (225ml) dry cider

Serves 4

Preheat oven to 375°F (190°F) gas mark 5.

Heat the oil in a heavy frying pan and sauté the garlic and onion until golden. Add the green pepper and courgettes, stir and gently sauté until softened. Pour the mixture into a casserole dish and add the remaining ingredients. Mix well, cover and bake for 40 minutes.

It is very important that the kidney beans are cooked thoroughly before being used in this recipe,

RED BEAN ENCHILLADAS

Enchilladas are tortillas, Mexican cornmeal pancakes, stuffed with a bean, vegetable or cheese filling and baked with a sauce and cheese. Tortillas are not difficult to make but obtaining the right ingredients for authenticity is not always easy, so do substitute shop bought tortillas for those given in the recipe if you wish, or make 100 per cent wholemeal tortillas.

2 tablespoons (30ml) butter or margarine
12fl oz (350ml) water, boiling
4½oz (125g) cornmeal
5oz (150g) wholemeal flour

Filling
2 tablespoons (30ml) vegetable oil
1 onion, finely diced
1 green pepper, seeded, finely chopped
2 tablespoons (30ml) finely chopped parsley
1lb (450g) cooked red kidney bear (about 8oz/225g uncooked)
½ teaspoon (2.5ml) ground cumin
½ teaspoon (2.5ml) chilli powder
Salt to taste
1¼ pints (750ml) tomato sauce
4½oz (100g) Cheddar cheese, grated

To make the tortillas stir the butter or margarine into the boiling water in a mixing bowl and then stir in the cornmeal. Set it aside to cool to room temperature and then mix in the wholemeal flour. Knead the dough for a few minutes adding more water if it is too stiff and more flour if it is too soft.

Now divide the dough into 12 portions and roll each into a ball. Flatten each ball on a lightly floured board and roll it out to about 6 in (15cm) diameter circle. Flour the rolling pin and board as necessary to stop the dough sticking. Heat an 8 in (20cm) ungreased non-stick or heavy frying pan over a medium to high heat and cook the tortillas one at a time for about 1 minute each side or until lightly flecked brown on both sides. Stack them and cover with a cloth to keep them warm and pliable.

If the tortillas are not to be used immediately, they can be softened for filling by heating them for a few seconds,on each side, in a hot frying pan.

When making the filling heat the oil in a saucepan and sauté the onions for 2 minutes. Add the green pepper and parsley and sauté for a further 2 minutes. Add the kidney beans, cumin, chilli powder and salt to taste. Add one third of the tomato sauce and bring the mixture to the boil. Cover, reduce heat and simmer for 5 minutes. Remove from the heat.

Preheat oven to 180°C (350°F) gas mark 4. Put 2-3 tablespoons (30-40ml) of filling onto each of the tortillas and roll them up. Grease a baking dish and place in it the filled tortillas, seam-side down, all in one layer if possible.

Pour over the remaining tomato sauce and sprinkle the cheese over the top. Bake in the preheated oven for 30 minutes or until the cheese starts to brown and the sauce bubbles. Serve immediately.

ARABIAN APPLE BEAN POT

1lb (450g) butter beans, soaked overnight and drained
2½pt (1.375l) water
2 tablespoons (30ml) vegetable oil or butter
2 medium onions, sliced
2 medium cooking apples, cored and sliced
½ teaspoon (2.5ml) turmeric
½ teaspoon (2.5ml) ground allspice
½ teaspoon (2.5ml) ground cinnamon
Salt and black pepper to taste
2fl oz (225ml) yoghurt
2oz (50g) dried apricots, chopped

Serves 6

Fit for a sheik The complementary flavours in this Arabian apple and bean pot create an exotic, warming dish. It is perfect served with yoghurt and chopped apricots.

Put the beans and water in a heavy saucepan and bring to the boil. Cover, reduce the heat and simmer until the beans are tender – about 1½ hours.

Meanwhile, heat the oil in a large, heavy frying pan and sauté the onions until golden. Add the apple, turmeric, allspice and cinnamon and cook, stirring, until the apple is softened.

Drain the beans and reserve the cooking liquid. Add the beans to the frying pan with just enough cooking liquid to wet the contents of the pan. Season to taste with salt and black pepper and simmer for 10 minutes.

Serve with a bowl of yoghurt and chopped apricots.

VIRGINIA BLACK-EYED BEANS

1lb (450g) black-eyed beans, soaked overnight and drained
1 medium onion, quartered
½ teaspoon (2.5ml) dried thyme
1 bay leaf
2 whole cloves
½ teaspoon (1.25ml) black pepper
Water
Salt to taste
Serves 4

Put the beans, onion, thyme, bay leaf, cloves and black pepper into a heavy saucepan. Just cover with water and bring to the boil. Cover, reduce the heat and simmer for 1 to 1½ hours or until peas are very tender. During the cooking time, check occasionally and add water as required. Season to taste with salt and serve.

WHOLE LENTIL PILAU

4 tablespoons (60ml) vegetable oil
8oz (225g) brown rice
24fl oz (600ml) boiling water
8oz (225g) green or brown lentils, soaked 4 to 6 hours, drained
½ teaspoon (2.5ml) allspice
Salt and black pepper to taste
1 clove garlic, crushed
2 medium onions, diced
8fl oz (225ml) yoghurt

Heat half the vegetable oil in a heavy saucepan and add the rice. Stir-fry for two to three minutes and then add the boiling water. Stir in the lentils, allspice and season to taste with salt and black pepper. Cover the pan, reduce heat and simmer until all the water is absorbed and both the rice and lentils are tender (approximately 25 minutes). Add more water if necessary.

Meanwhile, put the remaining oil in a heavy frying pan and sauté the garlic and onion until golden. Put the cooked rice and lentils into a serving bowl, garnish the top with the fried onions and garlic and pour over the yoghurt. Serve.

NUTS

Nuts are the fruits of certain trees and bushes. They normally consist of a hard or tough outer shell, which encloses the edible kernel. It is this kernel that we generally refer to as the nut.

Although they are best known as a snack food, nuts are a delicious, highly concentrated food with a wide range of cooking possibilities. They are a valuable source of proteins, vitamins, minerals, fats and fibre and may be used as an alternative to meat, fish, eggs or pulses. For more information about them, see the general introduction.

This chapter includes a wide variety of nut-based recipes, from burgers and kromeskies or croquettes through to pilau, casseroles and flans, using various types of nuts, such as pistachios, walnuts, brazils and hazelnuts (filberts).

NUT KROMESKIES

A 'kromeskie' is another name for a croquette. Serve kromeskies with a cheese sauce, some rice and a salad.

1oz (25g) Brazil nuts
2oz (50g) walnut pieces
3oz (75g) hazelnuts
1 medium onion, finely chopped
3oz (75g) carrots, peeled and grated
4oz (100g) fresh wholemeal breadcrumbs
1 tablespoon (15ml) finely chopped parsley
1 teaspoon (5ml) caraway seeds
Pinch of ground nutmeg
Salt and pepper to taste
2 eggs, beaten
Wholemeal flour for coating
2oz (50g) natural bran
Vegetable oil for deep frying
Cheese sauce

Serves 4

Put all the nuts on a baking sheet and lightly brown them under a moderate grill. Remove any skins from the nuts by rubbing them between the ends of a dry cloth.

Chop the nuts finely and mix them with the onion, carrots, breadcrumbs, parsley, caraway seeds, nutmeg, salt and pepper. Stir in half the beaten egg and stir well.

Divide the mixture into 8 equal portions and shape each into ovals. Coat each kromeski in flour, followed by beaten egg and the natural bran. Heat the oil and deep-fry the nut kromeskies for 5 to 8 minutes or until golden brown.

Nutritious nuts These tasty, protein-packed nut kromeskies make delicious snacks. Serve them with a cheese sauce for a sustaining meal.

MUSHROOM AND HAZELNUT CROUSTADE

A croustade – the dish originated in French cooking – is a sort of upside-down crumble, which comes covered with a sauce on top. This one is extremely tasty.

4oz (100g) wholemeal breadcrumbs
4oz (100g) hazelnuts, roasted and crushed
4oz (100g) flaked almonds
1 clove garlic, crushed
1 teaspoon (5ml) chopped fresh mixed herbs or ½ teaspoon (2.5ml) dried mixed herbs
2oz (50g) vegetable margarine

Serves 4

Sauce

1 large onion, chopped
1lb (450g) mushrooms, chopped
3 tablespoons (45ml) vegetable oil
2oz (50g) wholemeal flour
1 tablespoon (15ml) tahini
3 tablespoons (45ml) soya sauce
8fl oz (225ml) soya milk, diluted with 8fl oz (225ml) water
2 tablespoons (30ml) chopped parsley to garnish

Preheat oven to 425°F (220°C) gas mark 7.

Combine the breadcrumbs, hazelnuts, almonds, garlic and herbs. Mix well and rub in the margarine.

Press the mixture down well into a Swiss-roll tin. Bake for 20 minutes in the hot oven. Meanwhile make the sauce. Sauté the onion and mushrooms in the oil for five minutes. Stir in the flour and then the tahini and soya sauce; finally stir in the soya milk very slowly.

Remove the croustade from the oven. Allow to cool slightly, then pour over the sauce, garnish with parsley and serve.

RED CABBAGE AND CHESTNUT

This dish makes an extremely satisfying and nutritious main meal on a cold winter's night, especially if served with baked potatoes hot from the oven and a suitable seasonal salad. The chestnuts and apples combine to give the dish a distinctive flavour that is all its own.

If you want to make a slightly richer version of the recipe, add around 8fl oz (225ml) of fresh cream to the cabbage and chestnut just before you serve it.

2 medium onions, sliced
2 tablespoons (30ml) vegetable oil
½ medium red cabbage, finely chopped
Salt and black pepper to taste
6oz (175g) parboiled and peeled chestnuts
1lb (450g) apples, peeled thinly sliced
1 clove
Juice of 1 lemon

Serves 6-8

In a heavy saucepan, sauté the onions in the oil until golden. Add the cabbage, cover the pot and cook gently until the cabbage is softened. Season to taste with salt and black pepper, cover again and leave to simmer for five minutes. Add the chestnuts, apples, clove and lemon juice and leave to simmer, covered for about 20 minutes until all the vegetables are tender. Serve with baked potato and salad.

HAZELNUT AND VEGETABLE BURGERS

Served in wholemeal rolls or pitta bread, these burgers are delicious, nutritious and filling

2 carrots, finely grated
1 onion, finely chopped
2 sticks celery, finely chopped
4oz (100g) cabbage, finely grated
1 clove garlic, crushed
2oz (50g) hazelnuts, roasted and ground
2 tablespoons (30ml) wheatgerm
2 tablespoons (30ml) wholemeal breadcrumbs, plus more for coating burgers
1 tablespoon (15ml) soya flour
1 teaspoon (5ml) dried mixed herbs
1 tablespoon (15ml) soya milk
1 tablespoon (15ml) tomato purée
2fl oz (50ml) water
Salt to taste
Vegetable oil for frying

Serves 4

Mix together the carrots, onion, celery, cabbage, garlic, nuts, wheatgerm, breadcrumbs, soya flour and herbs. Whisk the soya milk, tomato purée and water together and stir the mixture into the dry ingredients. Season with salt and form the mixture into four burgers. Coat them in breadcrumbs and shallow-fry until golden brown on both sides or bake on a greased baking sheet for 20-30 minutes in preheated oven at 350°F (180°C), gas mark 4.

Family favourites Delicious, juicy hazelnut and vegetable burgers make a popular family meal when served with wholemeal rolls, mayonnaise and salad.

VEGETABLE CASSEROLE

A simple but wholesome dish which is easy to make. Try it also using different vegetables than given here or with the addition of herbs and spices to your own taste.

2 tablespoons (30ml) vegetable oil
1 medium onion, diced
1 small carrot, grated
4oz (100g) Chinese cabbage or spinach, shredded
2oz (50g) bean sprouts
4oz (100g) walnuts, chopped
½ teaspoon (2.5ml) hot pepper sauce
Soy sauce to taste
1lb (450g) cooked long-grain brown rice
2 eggs, beaten

Serves 4

Preheat the oven to 350°F (180°C) gas mark 4.

Heat the oil in a large, heavy pan, then add the onions and sauté them until soft. Stir in the carrot and cook over a moderate heat a further 2 minutes. Add the cabbage or spinach, mix well, cover the pan and cook for a few more minutes until the greens are wilted. Stir in the bean sprouts, walnuts, hot pepper sauce, soy sauce and cooked rice, mix well and then stir in the beaten egg. Turn the contents of the pan into a lightly greased casserole, cover and bake for 25 to 30 minutes. Serve hot.

NUT ROAST WITH TOMATO AND BASIL

This nut roast is excellent served with the special tomato sauce given in the recipe below. Make the sauce while the nut roast is cooking. If fresh basil is unavailable, make the basic tomato sauce given on page 114.

1oz (25g) butter
4oz (100g) onion, finely chopped
2oz (50g) Brazil nuts, finely chopped
2oz (50g) hazelnuts, finely chopped
4oz (100g) unsalted peanuts
4oz (100g) fresh brown breadcrumbs
2 eggs, beaten
4oz (100g) grated cheddar cheese
Salt and pepper

Sauce
8 large ripe tomatoes, skinned
1 small onion, finely chopped
½oz (15g) butter
Pinch of sugar
5 basil stalks
Salt and pepper
10 basil leaves, finely chopped

Serves 4-6

Preheat the oven to 350°F (180°C) gas mark 4.

Melt the butter in a large saucepan and sauté the onion in it until golden brown. Mix in the nuts, breadcrumbs, eggs and cheese and season well with salt and pepper.

Grease a 1½-lb (700g) loaf tin. Press the nut mixture evenly into the tin. Bake in the preheated oven for about 45 minutes or until golden brown.

Meanwhile, make the sauce. Cut the tomatoes into quarters and remove the seeds. Chop the flesh roughly. Saute the onion in the butter until soft and transparent. Add the chopped tomato, the pinch of sugar and the basil stalks. Cook over a low heat until most of the liquid has evaporated. Remove from the heat. Remove basil stalks, season with salt and pepper and add the chopped basil leaves and heat through.

Cool the nut roast for a few minutes before turning it out of the tin. Pour the sauce over the roast and serve.

NUT, CORN AND CHEESE CASSEROLE

8oz (225g) sweet corn
8oz (225g) tinned tomatoes
8oz (225g) chopped nuts
8oz (225g) cottage cheese
Paprika and salt to taste
2oz (50g) breadcrumbs
2 tablespoons (30ml) butter

Preheat oven to 350°F (180°C) gas mark 4.

Grease a casserole dish and put in separate layers of sweet corn, tomatoes, nuts and cottage cheese and season each layer with paprika and salt. Sprinkle breadcrumbs over the top and dot with butter. Bake for 30 minutes and serve.

TURKISH PISTACHIO PILAU

Serve this delicious Middle Eastern dish with a salad and some American round bread (page 57) or some pitta bread (page 55).

8oz (225g) butter or margarine
1½ (675g) lb rice
2½ (5ml) pt stock
1 teaspoon (5ml) allspice
½ teaspoon (2.5ml) cinnamon
Salt and black pepper to taste
2oz (50g) sultanas
4oz (100g) shelled pistachios

Serves 4

Melt the butter in a heavy frying pan or saucepan and sauté the rice in it until each grain is coated with butter. Add the stock, allspice, cinnamon and salt and black pepper and bring to the boil. Cover, reduce heat and cook for 20-25 minutes or until the rice is tender and all the liquid is absorbed.

Stir in the sultanas and half the pistachios, re-cover and set aside for five minutes.

Meanwhile, lightly toast the remaining pistachios under a grill. Pile the pilau on a heated serving dish and garnish with the toasted pistachios.

COURGETTE AND HAZELNUT FLAN

This is a flan with a difference – it has no pastry. If you do want to make the traditional variety, line an 8-9in (20-22.5cm) flan dish with 8oz (225g) shortcrust pastry. Pour into the greased flan dish and bake for 40 minutes in a 325°F (170°C) gas mark 3 oven.

1lb (450g) courgettes sliced
4oz (100g) chopped or ground hazelnuts
4 eggs, beaten
6oz (175g) grated cheese
1 teaspoon (5ml) dried basil
Salt and black pepper to taste

Preheat oven to 325°F (170°C) gas mark 3.

Put the courgettes in a heavy saucepan, add a little water, cover and steam for five-eight minutes until just softened.

Combine the softened courgettes with the hazelnuts, beaten egg, grated cheese, basil and salt and black pepper to taste. Pour the mixture into a greased flan dish and bake for 30 to 40 minutes.

WALNUT AND POTATO PATTIES

12oz (350g) mashed potato
6oz (175g) finely chopped walnuts
4oz (100g) fine breadcrumbs
1 teaspoon (5ml) mixed herbs
Grated rind of ½ lemon
2 tablespoons (30ml) finely chopped onion
Salt and black pepper to taste
8fl oz (225ml) milk, chilled
Oil for frying

Combine the first 7 ingredients and add enough milk to form a malleable mixture. Form into 4 round patties. Fry golden brown in hot oil or deep fry.

These patties are delicious served with béchamel sauce.

NUT AND CHEESE LOAF

8oz (225g) breadcrumbs
8fl oz (225ml) milk
8oz (225g) chopped nuts
8oz (225g) grated cheese
1 small onion, finely diced
1 tablespoon (15ml) chopped fresh parsley
1 egg, beaten
½ teaspoon (5ml) cayenne powder
1 teaspoon (5ml) salt

Preheat oven to 375°F (190°C) gas mark 5.

Soak the breadcrumbs in the milk and combine them with the remaining ingredients. Mix well and turn the mixture into a greased bread tin. Bake for 30 minutes or until the loaf is firm and lightly browned on top.

Spiced rice The distinctive taste of pistachio nuts brings an unusual flavour to this Turkish pilau.

EGG AND CHEESE DISHES

Eggs and cheese play an invaluable role in most cooks' repertoires. Both are important sources of nutrients – they are good value protein foods as well.

There is an almost limitless variety of cheeses available from all over the world. Goat's and ewe's milk cheeses, too, are becoming increasingly widely available. They have a distinctive flavour and are well worth looking out for and experimenting with in your cooking.

ITALIAN HERB PANCAKES

2oz (50g) flour
½-1 teaspoon (2.5-5ml) salt
2 eggs, beaten
2 tablespoons (30ml) melted butter
¼ pint (150ml) milk
(50g) frozen spinach, finely chopped
2 tablespoons (30ml) finely chopped fresh tarragon, basil or chives
Butter or oil for cooking
2-4 tablespoons (30-60ml) freshly grated Parmesan cheese
½ pint (300ml) Tomato Sauce

Cheese Filling
2x8oz (225ml) cartons cottage cheese
8 tablespoons (120ml) sour cream
2 eggs, beaten
2oz (50ml) freshly grated Gruyère cheese
2-4 tablespoons (30-60ml) freshly grated Parmesan cheese
2-4 tablespoons (30-60ml) finely chopped fresh herbs (parsley, chives, tarragon)
Salt and freshly ground black pepper
Grated nutmeg

Serves 4-6

Make crêpes. Combine the flour, salt, eggs and dry ingredients in a blender or food processor and add the melted butter and milk gradually to avoid lumps; beat into a smooth batter. The batter should be as thick as single cream (add a little water if it is too thick). Add finely chopped spinach and chopped fresh herbs and mix together well. Leave batter to stand for at least two hours before cooking the crêpes.

Heat an 8in (20cm) frying pan, add a small knob of butter and cover the bottom of the pan with a film of butter. As soon as it sizzles, pour 2 tablespoons (30ml) batter into the pan and tilt the pan to coat the bottom completely.

Cook over medium-high heat for a minute or two until crêpe is coloured and slightly crisp underneath; then flip it over with a palette knife and cook for a further one or two minutes. Repeat with the remaining batter, stacking the crêpes on top of each other with a piece of greaseproof paper between each one. Grease the pan lightly for each crêpe.

Make the cheese filling. In a large mixing bowl, combine first six ingredients and mix well. Add salt, freshly ground

black pepper and grated nutmeg, to taste. Refrigerate for at least one hour before using.

Spread each crêpe generously with filling (4 to 5 tablespoons (60-70ml) to each crêpe). Roll up each one and put them in a well-buttered rectangular baking dish. Chill for until one hour before using.

When ready to serve, brush each pancake with melted butter; sprinkle with freshly grated Parmesan cheese and bake for 20 minutes in a moderate 350°F (180°C) gas mark 4 oven. Serve with Tomato Sauce.

MIDDLE EASTERN CREPES

Ataif are paper-thin pancakes which are traditionally filled with a type of clotted cream (eishta) made from buffaloes' milk. I have substituted a highly spiced cheese filling and give a variation for sweet pancakes for serving as dessert.

Batter
10oz (275g) plain flour, sifted
3 eggs
1 tablespoon (15ml) rosewater
12fl oz (350ml) milk
½ teaspoon (2.5ml) salt
2 tablespoons (30ml) melted butter
Butter for frying

Filling
1lb (450g) Cheddar cheese, grated
2 tablespoons (30ml) lemon juice
¼ teaspoon (1.25ml) salt
½ teaspoon (2.5ml) cinnamon
¼ teaspoon (1.25ml) nutmeg

Serves 4-6

Make the batter. In a blender or food processor, combine the flour, eggs, rosewater, milk, salt and melted butter and beat into a smooth batter. Set aside to chill for at least one hour.

Combine all the filling ingredients and mix them well together. Preheat oven to 180°C (350°F) gas mark 4.

Stir the batter again. Heat ¼ teaspoon (1.25ml) butter in an 8in (20cm) frying pan. Spoon in a small amount of batter and tilt the pan to coat the bottom completely. Cook until the edges start to just brown. Turn the crêpe over, cook the other side until very slightly browned; remove it from the pan. Repeat until all the batter is used up, making about 12-16 crêpes. Stack the cooked crêpes on a plate and keep warm in the oven.

Put a heaped spoonful of the cheese filling onto the centre of each crêpe and roll it up, tucking in the edges. Heat ½ teaspoon (2.5ml) butter in the frying pan and fry the stuffed crêpes three or four at a time until nicely browned on both sides and with the cheese stuffing just melting. Add more butter before frying each batch. If you wish to serve them all at once, keep the cooked crêpes in the hot oven while you prepare the remainder.

Sweet Crêpes

8fl oz (225ml) whipped cream
4oz (100g) broken walnuts

Spread some of the cream and a sprinkling of walnuts over each of the cooked pancakes. Roll them up and serve garnished with more cream.

STUFFED PALATSCHINKEN

Palatschinken are Austrian pancakes very similar to the French crêpes or the Hungarian Palacsinta. Here I have stuffed them with a cheese and spinach filling and then baked them in a sour cream sauce.

Batter
8oz (225g) plain flour
2 eggs
6fl oz (175ml) milk
6fl oz (175ml) water
1/4 teaspoon (1.25ml) salt
Butter for frying the pancake

Filling
2oz (50g) butter
1 onion, finely diced
1lb (450g) fresh spinach, washed and finely chopped or 8oz (225g) frozen spinach, thawed, drained, finely chopped
8oz (225g) cottage cheese, drained
1 egg, beaten
Salt and freshly ground black pepper to taste

Sauce
8fl oz (225ml) sour cream
2 egg yolks

Serves 4

Make the batter. Combine the flour, eggs, milk, water and salt in a blender or food processor and beat into a smooth batter. Set aside to chill for at least one hour

Make the filling. Melt the butter in a pan and sauté the onion until just soft. Add the chopped spinach, cover and cook over a low heat until the spinach is wilted and tender. Remove the pan from the heat, transfer the contents to a bowl; leave to cool and then drain off any liquid. Mix in the cheese, egg and salt and black pepper to taste.

Preheat oven to 350°F (180°C) gas mark 4.

Heat an 8in (20cm) frying pan, add a small knob of butter and cover the bottom of the pan with a film of butter. As soon as it sizzles pour 2-3 tablespoons (30-45ml) batter into the pan and tilt the pan to coat the bottom completely. As soon as the pancake starts to bubble on top, turn it over and cook on the other side for less than 10 seconds. Remove the pancake from the pan and repeat with the remaining batter to make about 8-10 pancakes.

Divide the filling between the prepared pancakes and roll them up. Butter a baking dish and place the filled pancakes in it in a single layer. Mix together the egg yolks and sour cream and pour the mixture over the pancakes. Bake in the oven for 15 minutes. Serve immediately.

You will find that, in common with many Middle European dishes, these pancakes make a meal in themselves. If you want an accompaniment, try a plain green side salad.

Original omelettes These omelette dishes prove that a simple meal need not be a dull one. Courgette eggah (left) can be served as a main dish with salad, or cut into small pieces as an hors d'oeuvre. The buckwheat omelette (right) makes a tasty snack.

COURGETTE EGGAH

This Middle Eastern omelette, is firm, thick and well filled, not at all like a European omelette. Eggah is served like a pie, cut into wedges, or into squares if straight-edged (for hors d'oeuvres it can be cut into very small pieces). Serve as a main dish with salad, or as hors d'oeuvre.

4oz (100g) butter
1 large onion, finely chopped
2 cloves garlic, crushed
1lb (450g) courgettes, thinly sliced
9 eggs, lightly beaten
2 tablespoons (30ml) fresh parsley, finely chopped
½ teaspoon (2.5ml) turmeric
Salt and freshly ground black pepper to taste

Serves 4-6

Melt half the butter in a heavy frying pan and sauté the onion and garlic until softened. Add the courgettes and cook, stirring, over a medium heat until the courgettes are lightly browned and all the liquid has evaporated from the pan. Allow the mixture to cool and transfer it to a bowl.

Stir in the eggs, parsley, turmeric and salt and black pepper to taste. Preheat oven to 375°F (190°C) gas mark 5.

Melt the remaining butter and brush it over the inside of a 9in (23cm) non-stick casserole. Pour the egg mixture in and bake for 30 minutes or until nicely set. Remove the dish from the oven and if you wish, brown the top under a hot grill. Allow to cool. Turn the eggah onto a serving dish and cut it into thin wedges.

SPINACH ROULADE WITH CHEESE FILLING

2oz (50g) butter
12oz (350g) fresh spinach, washed, drained and chopped
or 6oz (175g) frozen spinach, defrosted and chopped
2oz (50g) wholemeal flour
16fl oz (450ml) milk
Salt and freshly ground black pepper
4 eggs
2 medium onions, finely sliced
4oz (100g) Cheddar cheese, grated
½ teaspoon (2.5ml) ground nutmeg
½ teaspoon (2.5ml) English mustard powder

Serves 4-6

Make the roulade. Melt half the butter in a saucepan over a low heat. Add the spinach and cook until the spinach is

French delicacy This mouth-watering spinach roulade with cheese filling combines delicate flavour and an appetising appearance. It makes a perfect light meal.

well wilted and all the watery liquid in the pan has evaporated.

Stir in half the flour and then slowly stir in one third of the milk. Bring the sauce to a gentle boil and cook, stirring, until it thickens. Season to taste with salt and pepper. Remove the pan from the heat. Leave the mixture to cool for five minutes. Preheat the oven to 400°F (200°C) gas mark 6.

Separate the egg whites from the yolks and whisk them stiff. Beat the egg yolks. Stir the egg yolks into the spinach sauce and then gently fold in the egg whites.

Line an 8in x 12in (20cm x 30cm) Swiss roll tin with greaseproof paper, leaving a good margin overlapping the edges of the tin. Pour the roulade batter in, spread it evenly over and bake in the oven for 25-30 minutes or until well set.

Meanwhile, make the filling. Melt the remaining butter in a pan over a moderate heat, add the onions and sauté until golden. Stir in the remaining flour, remove the pan from the heat and slowly stir in the remaining milk. Return the pan to the heat and bring to a gentle boil. Cook and stir until it thickens. Stir in the cheese, nutmeg, mustard and salt and pepper to taste and set on a very low simmer.

Remove the roulade from the oven, lift it out of the tin in the greaseproof paper. Spread half the filling over the top (keeping it away from the edges) and gently roll up the roulade using the paper to roll it over and get started. Serve the roulade with remaining filling poured over the top of the dish.

LITTLE OMELETTES

This is an Armenian dish, traditionally served at Easter but good at any time.

4 eggs
1 bunch parsley, finely chopped
1 bunch spring onions, finely chopped
1 clove garlic, crushed
Salt and black pepper to taste
4fl oz (100ml) vegetable oil

Serves 4

Beat the eggs and stir in all the other ingredients except the oil.

Heat the oil in a heavy frying pan and drop in tablespoonsful of the egg mixture.

Fill the pan but carefully keep each tablespoon of mixture separate from the next. Turn the little omelettes to brown both sides and remove them from the pan. Continue until all the mixture has been cooked. Serve hot or cold.

TORTILLAS WITH CHEESE FILLING

This dish can be served with or without a tomato sauce.

1 medium onion, finely diced
4 tablespoons (60ml) vegetable oil or melted butter
1lb (450g) Cheddar cheese, grated
2 tablespoons (30ml) finely chopped fresh parsley
¼ teaspoon (1.25ml) chilli powder
¼ teaspoon (1.25ml) ground cumin
Salt and black pepper to taste
8 wholemeal tortillas
Tomato sauce

Serves 4

Pockets of flavour Serve these crisp tortillas with cheese filling, with or without a tomato sauce for a delicious meal.

Preheat the oven to 375°F (190°C) gas mark 5.

Sauté the onion in half the oil or butter until softened. Add the cheese, parsley, chilli powder, cumin and seasoning to the onion mixture. Mix well.

Place a line of filling down each tortilla and then fold them over firmly. Place the stuffed tortillas on a greased baking dish and brush the tops with the remaining oil or butter. Now bake them, uncovered, in the preheated oven for 15 to 20 minutes or cover them with tomato sauce and bake them for 25 minutes.

CHATCHOUKA

Chatchouka is a dish of North African origin. Taken to Spain during the Arab invasions, it is said to be the forerunner of Spanish omelette.

2 tablespoons (30ml) vegetable oil
2 medium green peppers, cored, seeded, thinly sliced
½-1 red chilli pepper, finely chopped, optional
2 medium onions, diced
2 cloves garlic, crushed
18oz (525g) small tomatoes, halved
Salt and freshly ground black pepper to taste
6 medium eggs
Fresh parsley, finely chopped for garnishing

Serves 4

Heat the oil in a heavy frying pan and add the green peppers, chilli pepper, onions and garlic. Stir fry until the onion is softened and lightly coloured. Add the tomatoes and cook gently with occasional stirring until they are very soft. Season to taste with salt and black pepper.

Break the eggs over the surface of the contents of the frying pan and gently stir them with a wooden spoon to break the yolks. Cook, stirring occasionally, until the chatchouka is set. Serve garnished with parsley.

CAULIFLOWER WITH CHEESE SAUCE AND WALNUTS

1 large cauliflower, cut into large florets
1oz (25g) butter
1 medium onion, finely chopped
1oz (25g) wholemeal flour
10fl oz (275ml) hot milk
6oz (175g) Cheddar cheese, grated
2 teaspoons (10ml) prepared French mustard
Salt and black pepper to taste
4oz (100g) walnuts, lightly dry roasted

Serves 4-6

Cook the cauliflower in a little water or steam it until tender but still firm. Drain. Preheat the oven to 350°F (180°C) gas mark 4. Melt the butter in a saucepan and sauté the onion until softened. Stir in the flour and then gradually stir in the hot milk. Keep stirring until the sauce has thickened. Add the cheese slowly and finally the mustard and seasoning. Remove from the heat.

Put the cauliflower in a baking dish and pour the cheese sauce over the top. Bake for 15 minutes in the preheated oven. Remove and top the cauliflower with the walnuts. Continue baking for a further 15 minutes or until the dish has nicely browned.

SAUCES AND DRESSINGS

The following sauces can be served with vegetable or rice dishes, with salads, or just on their own with bread. Stuffed vegetables baked in tomato sauce are especially good. The tomato sauce is particularly versatile and is used in several recipes; the aubergine sauce makes use of the flesh from aubergines that have been hollowed out for stuffing. When making tahini sauces, always water with the tahini (if called for) before adding other liquids.

TOMATO SAUCE

2oz (50g) butter or vegetable oil
1 medium onion, finely diced
2lb (900g) fresh or tinned tomatoes (drained)
4 cloves garlic, crushed
1 medium green pepper, seeded, cored and diced
2 teaspoons (10ml) crushed, dried oregano
2 tablespoons (30ml) fresh parsley
1 bay leaf
Salt and pepper to taste

Makes about 1½ pt (850ml)

Melt the butter in a heavy saucepan or pour in the oil, and fry the onions over a low heat until soft.

Skin fresh tomatoes by dropping them in boiling water for a minute or two, then lift them out and peel off the skin. Alternatively use tinned tomatoes, drained. In either case chop the tomatoes into small pieces and add them, with the garlic and green pepper to the onions, stir well and simmer for 10 minutes.

Add the herbs and season to taste with salt and black pepper. Simmer for a further 10 minutes and allow to cool. Store in airtight jars, and pour a thin film of oil over the top of the sauce before screwing on the lid.

Variation

For a thicker, richer tomato sauce suitable for some types of pizza and the preparation of stuffings for vegetable and pasta dishes, add 6oz (175g) tomato purée with the chopped tomatoes.

BÈCHAMEL SAUCE

1oz (25g) butter
2 tablespoons (30ml) finely diced onion
1oz (25g) wholemeal flour
10fl oz (275ml) hot milk
Bay leaf
Pinch of nutmeg
Salt and freshly milled black pepper to taste

Makes about 14fl oz (400ml)

Melt the butter in a heavy saucepan over a lot heat. Add the onion and sauté until softened and transparent. Stir in the flour to form a smooth paste and cook, stirring, for 2 to 3 minutes. Slowly add the milk to the pan stirring constantly. Continue cooking and stirring until the sauce thickens. Add the bay leaf, nutmeg and salt and black pepper and simmer, covered, over a very lot heat for 10 minutes. Stir occasionally.

CHEESE SAUCE

Stir 2oz (50g) grated Cheddar cheese or other suitable cheese into the cooked Béchamel Sauce until it has melted. For extra flavour also stir in 1 teaspoon (5ml) prepared English mustard.

GARLIC AND WALNUT SAUCE

This sauce is very good with aubergine and courgette dishes.

4 cloves garlic
1 teaspoon (5ml) salt
2 tablespoons (30ml) breadcrumbs, dampened with a little water
4oz (100g) walnuts, finely chopped or ground
2 tablespoons (30ml) olive oil
Juice of 1 lemon

Makes about 00fl oz (00ml)

Crush the garlic and salt together in a bowl. Add the breadcrumbs and chopped walnuts to the garlic and salt and then crush the mixture into a paste. Add the olive oil drop by drop, whisking all the time. Repeat with the lemon juice.

TAHINI AND LEMON SAUCE

This sauce is excellent just on its own with bread, or as a salad dressing. Also serve it with rice and vegetable dishes and as a dip for mezze.

2 cloves garlic, crushed
1 teaspoon (5ml) salt
4fl oz (100ml) tahini
2fl oz (50ml) water
Juice of 2 lemons

Makes about 8fl oz (225ml)

Mash the garlic with the salt in a bowl. Slowly beat in the tahini, water and lemon juice in that order. Blend well.

Variation

Add 4oz (100g) chopped walnuts with the garlic and salt.

AUBERGINE CREAM SAUCE

Instead of whole aubergines, the flesh from aubergines that have been hollowed out for stuffing may be used in this recipe.

2 to 3 medium aubergines
2oz (50g) butter
3 tablespoons (45ml) flour
8fl oz (225ml) single cream
2oz (50g) grated cheese
Salt to taste
Grated peel of ½ a lemon

Slit the aubergines lengthwise and sprinkle salt in the cut. Set aside, cut side down, for 30 minutes, then rinse and drain.

Place the aubergines in a preheated 400°F (205°C) gas mark 5 oven for 20 minutes. Peel off the skin. Alternatively hold the aubergines, impaled one at a time on a skewer, over a gas flame and singe them all over until the skin bubbles and flakes off easily. Chop the aubergine flesh into small pieces.

Melt the butter in a heavy pan, stir in the flour, and cook, stirring, for 3 to 4 minutes. Add the aubergine flesh and beat to make a smooth mixture. Stir in the single cream and cheese and gently simmer, stirring, until the cheese is melted. Add salt to taste, mix in the lemon rind, and serve hot with vegetables.

If you use uncooked aubergine flesh rather than whole cooked aubergines, salt the flesh first, chop, rinse and then fry in a little butter before using it as described in the recipe.

CHILLI HOT PEANUT SAUCE

Sambals are hot and/or spicy Indonesian sauces or relishes which are served as accompaniments to other dishes. They form a very important part of an Indonesian meal, which in itself consists of many small dishes. Chilli peppers are the most common ingredient in these sauces and, consequently, sambals are often very hot and even fiery. They are served in very small bowls which sit on the table so that you can season your own food with the right amount for your taste. It's very much a question of personal choice about which sambals to serve with which dishes, but if you remember that sambals are chosen and added to enchance the dishes and not to overpower them, you won't go far wrong. Sambals can also be added in very small amounts to soups, sauces and dressings if they need a little extra bite.

Most sambals keep well and are useful to have around. They should be kept in sterilized, airtight containers and refrigerated.

Sambal Kacang, the first recipe, is a tasty but not too hot sauce. It also provides the basis for making other sambals (see variations below).

4oz (100g) roasted, unsalted peanuts
2 red chillies
2 cloves garlic
2 tablespoons (30ml) dark soya sauce
2 tablespoons (30ml) white vinegar
2 tablespoons (30ml) brown sugar

Serves 4

Put all the ingredients into a food processor or blender and blend them together until the mixture is smooth. If the mixture is too thick, add water, a tablespoon at a time, until the consistency is that of very thick mustard. Store unused sambal in an airtight jar in the refrigerator. It will keep for several weeks.

Variations

- Add 8oz (225g) scalded and peeled tomatoes to the ingredients and blend as above. Add salt if required.
- Add 4fl oz (100ml) fresh or canned coconut milk to the mixture during blending. Add salt as required. Store in an airtight jar in the refrigerator.
- Leave out the salt and add 1 tablespoon (5ml) prawn paste or 2 anchovy fillets during blending. Add salt at the end, if necessary.

DRESSINGS

Included here, too, are all the dressings called for in the recipes in the other sections of the book. As with the recipes themselves, the plan has been to present you with a wide choice. There are all types – from a basic oil and vinegar dressing to a creamier dressing made with tofu as well as a good, old-fashioned mayonnaise.

Starchy salads, particularly those containing beans, benefit from being dressed while they are still warm – this enables the flavourings to penetrate more deeply. Taste and add more dressing, if necessary, when the salads are cold.

Dressings are often the most expensive part of a salad, so to add too much is a waste of money. It can also spoil the taste of the salad if the salad's natural flavours are swamped by that of the dressing. Do make sure, however, that you mix in the dressing well or the amounts given here may not seem enough.

OILS AND VINEGARS FOR SALAD DRESSINGS

Well-flavoured oils and vinegars are essential for making tasty salad dressings. They provide their own taste and are the base for any additional flavourings such as herbs or spices.

THE STRONGLY-FLAVOURED OILS

Olive oil It is better to use a good olive oil with discretion than a poor one continuously. Good olive oil has a clean, fruity flavour without any aftertaste. Cold-pressed virgin oil of which the best grades are Virgin Extra Fine is the best one to choose. Always use a good olive oil on leaf salads.
Sesame oil A sweet, nutty flavoured oil, very good in association with shoyu (natural soya sauce) or for cooking aubergines. Buy the thick, brownish non-refined oil.
Walnut oil An alternative to olive oil on more robust green leaf salads. A strong nutty taste not to everyone's liking. Does not keep well, so buy in small amounts and keep in a cool place.

THE NEUTRAL OILS

By definition, these are going to be generally quite similar, though different brands of the same oil may taste different. Some will be clean tasting, others will have a considerable aftertaste. Try several and when you find the brand you like, stick to it.
Groundnut oil Much recommended by the prophets of the 'new cuisine'. Good examples have a light, mild flavour. Also known as peanut or arachide oil.
Safflower oil The ideal oil for anyone on a low-fat diet, for it is very high in polyunsaturates.
Sunflower oil A thin, mild oil high in polyunsaturates. Add a little olive oil if you want more flavour.

VINEGARS

Cider vinegar is the best all-round solution. It is more important that you have one good vinegar than a selection of inferior ones. This does not mean that yu should only ever use one sort of vinegar – if you like a certain specialist vinegar, keep that as well. Avoid malt vinegar and distilled spirit vinegars.

You can produce your own flavoured vinegars by infusing fresh herbs like marjoram, rosemary, tarragon or thyme for at least a week in small bottles of vinegar.

VINAIGRETTE DRESSING

Vary your vinaigrette dressings according to the ingredients they are to be served with. I find that heavy, dried bean or starchy rot vegetable salads may be best with a vinaigrette dressing with a 3 parts oil to 1 part vinegar ratio, while strongly flavoured greens are best with a 4 to 1 oil/vinegar ratio, and sweet, delicate lettuce is best with a 5 to 1 ratio.

I prefer to use a light olive oil but its flavour would be wasted if you were going to add strong spices to the dressing, so in that case, use peanut or sunflower oil instead. Mustard is the most usual addition to the basic vinaigrette. It serves a two-fold purpose; first to give 'bite' when used with rich or slightly sweet foods like avocados or root vegetables, and secondly it helps to emulsify the oil and vinegar so that the dressing clings to the salad instead of running off. If you are going to use chopped fresh herbs in the vinaigrette, add them just before you dress the salad.

4½fl oz (120ml) vegetable oil
2 tablespoons (30ml) wine vinegar, cider vinegar or lemon juice
Salt and pepper to taste
1 teaspoon (5ml) prepared mustard (optional)

Makes 150ml (5fl oz)

Place all ingredients in a bowl or liquidizer and beat or blend well. Test and adjust seasoning if necessary before you serve the dressing.

MAYONNAISE

Whatever you make and flavour mayonnaise with is a matter of personal taste and consideration for the vegetables which it is to accompany. For instance, delicate vegetables such as asparagus deserve a mayonnaise made from a light, cold-pressed virgin oil from Italy or Provence (method A). Mayonnaise to be thinned with yoghurt for, say, a potato or cabbage salad should be made with the whole egg and groundnut or sunflower oil (method B).

THE BASIC RULES FOR MAKING PERFECT MAYONNAISE

- Mayonnaise is much easy to make with fresh eggs.
- Ingredients and equipment must be warm. Some people warm everything in hot water.
- At first, add the oil very slowly.
- Don't use less than 5fl oz (150ml) of oil, or more than 10fl oz (300ml), per one large egg.
- The better quality of oil used, the less seasoning the mayonnaise will require.

METHOD A

1 large (size 2) egg yolk
1 teaspoon (2.5ml) Dijon mustard
a good pinch of salt
10fl oz (300ml) Italian extra virgin olive oil or Provencal oil
2 tablespoons (30ml) lemon juice to taste
Additional salt and black pepper to taste

OR

METHOD B

1 large egg
1 tablespoon (5ml) prepared mustard
Good pinch of salt
9fl oz (250ml) vegetable oil
2 tablespoons (30ml) wine vinegar to taste
Additional salt, black pepper, paprika or cayenne pepper to taste

Makes 300ml (½ pint)

Put the egg yolk (method A) or break the whole egg (method B) into a bowl or liquidizer goblet, add mustard and salt. Beat or blend at medium speed until the mixture thickens slightly. Still beating, pour in the oil from a measuring jug, drop by drop initially and then, as it begins to thicken, in a slow, but steady stream.

Carefully beat or blend in the lemon juice or wine vinegar and season to taste with the salt and pepper. Store in a cool place for no more than a day.

PEANUT DRESSING

1 clove garlic, crushed
1 small onion, diced
1 tablespoon (15ml) vegetable oil
4oz (100g) roasted (unsalted peanuts or 100g (4oz) peanut butter
1 teaspoon (5ml) brown sugar
1 tablespoon (15ml) lemon juice
8fl oz (225ml) water
Salt to taste

Makes 12fl oz (350ml)

Lightly brown the garlic and onion in the oil. Transfer the garlic, onion and frying oil to a blender or food processor and add all the other ingredients. Blend smooth. Transfer the dressing to a pan, bring to the boil and then simmer over a low heat, stirring for 5 minutes. Use immediately or allow to cool.

JAPANESE WHITE DRESSING

5oz (150ml) cake of tofu (bean-curd)
2 tablespoons (30ml) sesame seeds
1 tablespoon (15ml) white sugar
½ teaspoon (2.5ml) salt

Makes 150ml (5fl oz)

Remove excess water from the tofu in order to get a dressing of the right consistency. Wrap the tofu in 2 or 3 layers of absorbent kitchen paper and place a small bowl containing water on top of it. Leave for 30 minutes and then mash the pressed tofu in a bowl.

Dry-roast the sesame seeds over a moderate heat untl they are brown. Crush the seeds into a paste with a pestle and mortar and stir the paste into the tofu. Add the sugar and salt and stir into a smooth consistency.

VARIATION

- The crushed sesame paste may be replaced by tahini or Chinese sesame paste.
- For Vinegared White Dressing, stir in 2 teaspoons (10ml) rice or cider vinegar.

COCONUT DRESSING

A southeast-Asian dressing which is good on both cooked and uncooked vegetable salads.

4oz (100g) fresh coconut, grated or 4oz (100g) desiccated coconut moistened with 2 tablespoons (30ml) hot water
½small onion, finely diced
Pinch chilli powder or ⅛ teaspoon (0.5ml) hot pepper sauce
2 tablespoons (30ml) lemon juice

Makes 8fl oz (225ml)

Put all the ingredients into a blender or food processor and briefly pulse the machine to form a homogeneous but not completely smooth mixture.

JAPANESE MUSTARD DRESSING

1 teaspoon (5ml) prepared English mustard
2 tablespoons (30ml) rice vinegar or cider vinegar
1 tablespoon (15ml) shoyu (natural soy sauce)
1-2 teaspoons (5-10ml) sugar

Makes 4-5 tablespoons (70ml)

Combine the mustard, vinegar and soy sauce in a small mixing bowl, add sugar to taste and stir well to dissolve the sugar.

DESSERTS

Most people have their own firm favourites when it comes to the dessert course of a meal, so I have included just a few of my personal choices here.

Of course, the healthiest of all is fresh fruit salad. Try the variation on page 123 – Tropical Fruit Salad – as this is a luxurious and unconventional variation.

If you are anxious about cholesterol and calories, substitute yoghurt for cream. Though it contains fewer calories than double cream, you will find that Greek strained yoghurt tastes just as delicious.

Sweet alternatives These sweet mini-pancakes can be served with a variety of different sweet fillings, such as dates, cream or spiced chopped nuts, as shown here.

BAKLAVA

Baklava, made from layers of buttered filo pastry with a nut or sweet cheese filling, is the perennial pastry favourite of Middle Eastern cooking. This recipe makes rather a lot but the preparation is just as easy as for a few and the baklava will keep well for a week. If the pastries begin to dry out, pour a little more syrup over them.

2 egg whites
4oz (100g) caster sugar
1lb (450g) ground nuts (walnuts, almonds, pistachios, peanuts, hazelnuts etc or a mixture of these)
1 teaspoon (5ml) cinnamón
12oz (350g) sugar
8fl oz (225ml) water
Juice of 1 lemon
1 tablespoon (15ml) orange blossom or rose water
1lb (450g) filo pastry dough
8oz (225g) butter, melted

Makes 30-40 pastries

To make the filling, beat the egg whites stiff, slowly beat in the caster sugar and then fold in the nuts and cinnamon. Set the filling aside.

Dissolve the sugar in the water and lemon juice in a pan. Bring the mixture to the boil and simmer uncovered for 10-15 minutes until slightly thickened. Stir in the orange blossom or rose water and remove from the heat. Leave the syrup to cool to room temperature.

Preheat oven to 375°F (175°C) gas mark 4. Choose a large, not too deep baking tin about 12in by 16in (30cm by 40cm) and brush the sides and bottom with melted butter. Spread out one sheet of pastry and brush it with melted butter. Top with half the remaining sheets, brushing each of them with butter and fitting them into the tin one at a time, folding to fit as necessary.

Spread the filling evenly over the top. Brush the remaining sheets of pastry with melted butter and place them one at a time on top of the filling; again fold to fit.

With a sharp knife cut through all the layers of pastry diagonally both ways to form diamond shaped baklava.

Bake the baklava in the preheated oven for 30 minutes and then at 450°F (230°C) gas mark 7 for 15 minutes until the pastry is nicely browned.

Remove the baklava from the oven and immediately pour over the syrup. Set aside to cool in the tray.

For very moist baklava, pour two thirds of the syrup over the hot baklava. Allow to cool and then pour the remaining syrup (slightly chilled) over the baklava.

Variation

Sometimes the syrup is ommitted altogether and the baklava is served crisp and sprinkled with icing sugar.

Middle Eastern favourite
Baklava is a succulent pastry sweet, of Turkish origin, which is the perfect complement to good black coffee.

ARABIAN DOUGHNUTS WITH SYRUP

2 medium eggs
2 tablespoons (30ml) vegetable oil
2 tablespoons (30ml) orange blossom water
Grated rind of 1 small orange
About 8oz (225g) plain flour
2 teaspoons (10ml) bicarbonate of soda
Oil for deep frying

Syrup
1 lb (450g) sugar
12 fl oz (350ml) water
Juice of 1 lemon

Makes 8 doughnuts

In a mixing bowl, whisk the eggs, vegetable oil, orange blossom water and orange rind into a smooth liquid.

Sift together the flour and the bicarbonate of soda and slowly beat the mixture into the liquid. The dough should become thick enough to only just pour from a spoon. Add more flour if necessary. Cover and set aside in a warm place for 30 minutes.

Golden sweets These light, golden Arabian doughnuts absorb the rich syrup poured over them, to make a delicious dessert.

Meanwhile, prepare the syrup. Over a medium heat dissolve the sugar in the water, add the lemon juice and bring to the boil. Reduce heat and gently boil the syrup for 10 minutes. Set aside and allow to cool.

Heat the oil for deep frying, flour your hands and form the dough into small tomato-sized balls, flatten them slightly and then push a finger through the centre to form a hole. Prepare three at a time and deep fry them, turning until golden brown, about 4-5 minutes. Drain on paper towels and repeat for the remaining dough. Pour the the syrup liberally over the doughnuts – this is definitely a dish for people with a sweet tooth – and leave them for an hour to allow the syrup to soak in.

FRENCH PEAR TART

5oz (150g) plain flour
5oz (150g) wholemeal flour
½ teaspoon (2.5ml) salt
4oz (100g) butter, diced
2oz (50g) vegetable fat, diced
4oz (100g) soft brown sugar
2oz (50g) walnuts, finely chopped
2 egg yolks
2-4 tablespoons (30-60ml) iced water,
2oz (50g) honey
5 fl oz (150ml) water
4 large pears, peeled halved and cored
1 egg white, lightly beaten
2 tablespoons (30ml) caster sugar
Sour cream or yogurt to serve
Serves 4-6

First make the pastry. Sift the flour and salt together into a large bowl, add the fats and rub the mixture together until it resembles coarse breadcrumbs. Mix in the sugar and the walnuts. Add the egg yolks and enough chilled water to bind the mixture.

Place the honey and water in a saucepan large enough to hold all the pear halves in a single layer. Bring the syrup to the boil and simmer for 5 minutes. Add the pears to the syrup and gently simmer them for 10 to 15 minutes or until just tender. Remove them from the heat and let them cool.

Preheat the oven to 375°F (190°C) gas mark 5. Line a 9" (23cm) flan ring with two-thirds of the pastry. Drain the pears and place them in the pastry case with the broad end of the pears outwards and the cut sides down. Dampen the sides of the pastry with water and then cover the flan with the remaining pastry, pressing down slightly to reveal the shape of the pears. Seal the edges and crimp all round. Cut a small hole in the centre of the flan to allow steam to escape when the flan is baked. Brush the top of the flan with the beaten egg white and then sprinkle it with caster sugar.

Bake in the preheated oven for 30 to 35 minutes or until the pastry is golden and firm to touch. Cool. Carefully remove the flan from the ring and serve warm or cold with the sour cream or yogurt.

Perfect pâtisserie This succulent French pear tart is equally delicious hot or cold, served with yoghurt or sour cream.

SWEET PANCAKES (ATAIF)

Ataif are thin pancakes akin to the French cre^pes, but smaller in diameter. They can be made from both yeasted and unyeasted batter. Recipes for both are given here. Other suggestions for fillings are also given.

Choose one of the batters and select a filling or fillings, make the sweet syrup and finally, make the pancakes.

YEASTED WATER BATER

1 teaspoon (5ml) dry yeast
½ teaspoon (2.5ml) sugar
12fl oz (350ml) lukewarm water
12oz (350g) plain flour, sifted
¼ teaspoon (1.25ml) salt

Put the yeast, sugar and a little of the water in a bowl and whisk with a fork. Set aside in a warm place for about 15 minutes or until the mixture starts to bubble and then combine it with the remaining water.

Sift the flour and salt into a mixing bowl and form a well in the centre. Slowly pour in the yeast mixture and whisk to a smooth batter. Cover the mixture and set aside for an hour, by which time the batter should be bubbling and risen. This means it is ready for cooking.

UNYEASTED MILK BATTER

10oz (275g) plain flour, sifted
2 teaspoons (10ml) sugar
2 eggs, lightly beaten
2 tablespoons (30ml) melted butter
1 tablespoon (15ml) rosewater (optional)
12fl oz (350ml) milk

In a blender or food processor or mixing bowl combine all the ingredients and beat into a smooth batter. Set aside in the refrigerator for 1 hour.

To cook the pancakes barely cover the bottom of a heavy frying pan, about 6in (15cm) diameter, with oil, and heat until the oil is hot but not smoking. Spoon in 1-2 tablespoons (15-30ml) batter and tilt the pan to just coat the bottom completely with batter. Cook until the edges start to brown, then turn the pancake over and brown the other side. Stack the cooked pancakes on a plate in a warm oven.

Serve with one or more of the fillings suggested below.

FILLING FOR PANCAKES

- Whipped cream
- Chopped nuts
- Chopped nuts mixed with a little sugar and cinnamon
- Fresh dates
- Cream cheese sweetened with a little honey
- Sweet syrup (see Baklava)

Pineapple extravaganza The ingredients of this tropical fruit salad can be expensive, so save it for a special occasion to stun your guests.

FRESH FRUIT COMPOTE

As I have said in the introduction to this section, there is nothing as healthy as a pudding based on fresh fruit. This recipe is one of my personal favourites, especially with the variations I have suggested below.

The combination of fruit I have given here is only a suggestion, however. You are free to substitute any mixture of fruits, or a single fruit.

4oz (100g) sugar
16fl oz (450ml) water
2 peaches
2 tart apples, washed
8oz (225g) plums, washed, stoned and halved
8oz (225g) strawberries, washed
2 sticks cinnamon, or
1 teaspoon (5ml) ground cinnamon
Juice of 1 lemon

Serves 4

Put the sugar and water in a pan and bring to the boil. Set to simmer.

Plunge the peaches in a pan of boiling water and then immediately remove them and drop them into cold water. The skins will now come off easily. Slice the skinned peaches and the apples and put them into the simmering syrup. Add the plums, strawberries, cinnamon and lemon juice. Simmer for 15 minutes, stirring occasionally. Remove cinnamon sticks (if used). Leave to cool, chill, and serve with whipped cream.

Variations

If rosewater is available, add 1 or 2 drops to the simmering fruit. Try cardamom in place of the cinnamon for a different flavour.

Simply stunning
Any combination of fruits can be used in this refreshing fresh fruit compote. Serve with whipped cream.

TROPICAL FRUIT SALAD

Though this is quick to prepare and delicious, the ingredients can be expensive. Save this fruit salad for the occasional special meal.

½ ripe pineapple, peeled, cored and chopped
1 banana, sliced
2 kiwi fruits, peeled, halved and sliced
1 mango, peeled and chopped
1 tablespoon (15ml) lemon juice
¼ pint (150ml) grape juice

Serves 4

Mix together the pineapple, banana, kiwi fruit and mango. Pour the lemon and grape juice over the fruit and serve chilled, in the pineapple shell for extra effect if you wish.

ACKNOWLEDGEMENTS

The Paul Press would like to thank the following for their invaluable assistance in the preparation of this book.

Neal Street East, Covent Garden, London WC2 9PV; Elizabeth David, 46 Bourne Street, London SW1; David Mellor, 4 Sloane Square, London SW1; Rosenthal Studio Haus, 102 Brompton Road, London SW3; Graham and Green, 4 & 7 Elgin Crescent, London W11; Fieldhouse, 89 Wandsworth Bridge Road, London SW6